Contents

Acknowledgement.. 3

Introduction.. 4

Chapter 1- The Genesis..5

Chapter 2- Who Or What, Is a Witness? 18

Chapter 3- When Shall These Things Be? 33

Chapter 4- Sign Shall Follow the Believers.................43

Chapter 5- Dressed for The Occasion; Sackcloth 55

Chapter 6- Shut It Down; God is Talking 65

Chapter 7- Mr. Sun and Mrs. Moon 75

Chapter 8- Zechariah's Encounter 79

Chapter 9- Context-Matter-Break-Build- Spirit 91

Chapter 10- God The Everlasting Light- DNA 113

Chapter 11-Queue, Better Yet, Cue the Anointed

      Night light-moon 126

Chapter 12- Sun, Soaked and Anointed 134

Chapter 13- The Beast 139

Acknowledgement

Angie, Janet, Michael, thank you for being the destiny helpers that the Lord used to help me along the way. I appreciate the sacrifices, kindness, and painstaking dedication. I pray that He rewards you for your obedience. May your blessings never run out. Thank you from the bottom of my heart.

To my Eli- my Aunty G, Gloria Lightbody- You never birthed me, but you are the priest figure and mother that the Lord used to protect and take care of me, as A young child. You are the embodiment of pure love. You guided me when hearing from the Lord. There are not enough words to thank you, I love you and I dedicate this book to you. Thank you for nurturing me, loving me, and keeping me safe for the time I was in your care. Truly God is perfect in ALL His ways.

Introduction

In the mysterious and prophetic tapestry of the Book of Revelation, the imagery and symbolism woven into its verses have captivated the minds and hearts of believers for centuries. Among its enigmatic passages, the identity of the Two Witnesses has been a subject of much speculation and interpretation over the years. While traditional views often point to these witnesses as symbolic representations of prophetic figures or entities, a unique perspective emerges—one that unveils the celestial bodies that have long adorned the heavens with their radiant presence. In this groundbreaking book "Apocalyptic Lights: Revelation of the Two Witnesses" we embark on a journey of exploration and revelation into the cosmic significance of the Sun and the Moon as the two witnesses foretold in these apocalyptic visions of John while he was on the Island of Patmos. Through a lens that dares to challenge conventional interpretations, we will delve into what was considered symbolism and prove that the holy writings in Revelation 11 are actual, literal, spiritual truths, embedded in the celestial realm. Revealing a new perspective and shedding new light on the enduring mysteries of this ancient text.

"The entrance of Your words gives light; It gives understanding to the simple. I opened my mouth and panted, For I longed for Your commandments. Look upon me and be merciful to me, As Your custom is toward those who love Your name. Direct my steps by Your word, And let no iniquity have dominion over me". Psalm 119: 130-134

⭐ CHAPTER 1- THE GENESIS

Let me begin by saying, what you are about to read may be considered "different", or unusual. Some may agree, while others may not. Like any other body of prophetic writings, read and pray for revelation and light.

HOW DID I GET HERE?

This revelation was made known to me in April of 2020, while still living in Waterbury, CT, before being instructed by the Lord to move. It was an unusually windy night. The breeze was howling and blowing at such a speed that it made the entire house shake. It did not frighten me, because this was at a time when the entire world was already shaken by Covid and the large amount of death that was mounting daily. So, this was nothing to me, I was prepared for the unexpected to happen at any moment. In fact, this phenomenon happening outside intrigued me somehow.

I couldn't remember ever hearing the wind whistle so loud, meanwhile feeling the effects of the whirlwind, at the same time. The intensity of the wind was so loud and powerful that it could not be ignored. It felt as though we were in a tornado. As if the house would immediately be taken up, or crumble at any moment. I knew this was significant. I immediately started to pray. My prayers felt distanced.

"Commit thy way unto the Lord; trust also in him; and he shall bring it to pass. ⁶ And he shall bring forth thy righteousness as the light, and thy judgment as the noonday". Psalm 37: 5-6

I couldn't stop thinking of the wind. Somehow, I was pulled closer to the window, where I started to pray again. Even then, I felt far from God. I felt as though I needed to be closer, so I went outside.

Now I know going out in that type of weather was probably not the most logical thing to do at that moment, but then, nothing in the spiritual world is logical.

The sky was clear, and the wind was ferociously blowing. I wanted to talk to God amid the howling and uncontrollable wind.

I felt a drawing, a yearning, a pulling, a desire to be under the heavens talking with my Father. The sky, the wind, the howls were all mesmerizing. I closed my eyes and just started to commune with Him. I felt His presence and basked in His presence outside in my back yard. During the howls there was such peace, such a sweet, safe, intimate connection. While communing with Him right there outside, not only did I feel an immense peace come over me, but I also realized that the wind was calming down. The wind was no longer bolstering, but now just a calm, slight breeze. It was then that I looked up at the big, beautiful moon. I hadn't noticed it before. It was as if time stood still. I felt as though my prayers were heard, not only by God, but by a silent observer. At that moment I realized that the moon was recording everything that had just taken place. I realized that the moon was watching everything as it was happening. Not just with me, but with everyone, everywhere. It took a moment to sink in, but it was revealed to me at that very moment that the Two Witnesses had been here all this time.

"The LORD is my light and my salvation— whom shall I fear? The LORD is the stronghold of my life— of whom shall I be afraid?" Psalm 27:1

Needless to say, I was blown away. This wasn't the first time the Lord had shown me things, just not things of this magnitude. Of course I shrugged it off, and even chuckled at the thought. Could the answer really be hidden in plain sight and completely

overlooked? Could it be that the Two Witnesses are already evident, just not yet appointed for ministry? Could it be that the Two Witnesses are here, but the appointed

time to work has not yet come? The questions started flooding my mind, one after the other. My mind was overwhelmed with questions that first trickled in, then bombarded me like a tsunami.

As the questions came, the answers started to trickle in little by little, one by one. This was big. In fact, this was very big. Who would believe me? This was crazy, insane, mind baffling. I'm going to sound crazy. I laughed out loud, over and over again. The Lord has a way where He just gets our attention, and we can't do anything about it. Like it or not. In any case, most prophets and prophecy were considered crazy, so I was in good company. This would require research, getting into the Word, and intense communication with the Holy Spirit. This was quite a feat. While the revelation was made known to me on that windy night, that the sun and the moon are indeed the two witnesses, proving that would take some work. I shared it with one friend who laughed, and who could blame her? I even laughed, until I cried. Then I laughed again.

"And the light shineth in darkness; and the darkness comprehended it not". John 1:5

As time went on, I realized that this was no laughing matter, and that this assignment was given specially to me, to share with others. The Lord shared with me something incredibly sacred, and it was my responsibility and assignment to share it, for His glory. So, in obedience and by leading of the Holy Spirit, I am sharing with you.

Join me as we traverse the celestial pathways of the heavens, where the sun, with its life-giving warmth and illuminating brilliance, and the moon, with its gentle glow and mystical allure, take center stage as heralds of divine messengers and bearers of cosmic testimony. Together, we will unravel the veils of symbolism, literalism and allegory, and unveil the hidden truths that lie beyond the surface of this captivating narrative.

Please join me as we navigate the celestial spheres and traverse the eschatological landscape of Revelation. Let us open our minds to the possibility that the Sun and the Moon, the celestial luminaries that have guided humanity through the ages, may hold a deeper, more profound role in the grand narrative of God's unfolding plan for creation.

Prepare to embark on a transformative journey of discovery and illumination as we unlock the secrets of the celestial witnesses in Revelation.

Please pray, relax, and be prepared for an awakening as we delve into revealing what has been hidden in plain sight for so long.

"But if we walk in the light, as he is in the light, we have fellowship one with another, and the blood of Jesus Christ his Son cleanseth us from all sin". 1 John 1:7

IN THE BEGINNING

The Book of Genesis is a foundational Book that is found in the Torah and in the Bible. It tells of the creation of the universe, the world as we know it, and of man. Genesis 1 tells what happens "In the beginning".

King James Version, which we used mostly in this book, unless otherwise mentioned, tells us in Chapter 1 verse 1 and 2 that, *"In the beginning God created the heaven and the earth.² And the earth was without form, and void; and darkness was upon the face of the deep. And the Spirit of God moved upon the face of the waters".*

There was total and utter darkness until the creation of light, which is found in Genesis 1:3, *"And God said, Let there be light: and there was light".* In verse 4, the scripture goes on to tell us that, *"God saw that the light was good, and he separated the light from the darkness.".* It is important to note that THIS light is the all-encompassing light, that we will get into more in Chapter 9. This all-encompassing light, what scripture calls "True Light" is very important, so important that it is found at the top of each page within this book, as a gentle and loving reminder of His love, redemptive power, grace, and majesty. It is also important to point out that this all-encompassing light that was created in verses 3 and 4, was created prior to the creation of the luminous light that emanates from the sun and the moon.

"Thy word is a lamp unto my feet, and a light unto my path." Psalm 119:105

That luminous light, the sun and the moon, is what we will discuss in the body of this book. Let's move on to Genesis 1 verse 14-19 NIV and KJV, respectively.

> [14] And God said, "Let there be lights in the vault of the sky to separate the day from the night, and let them serve as signs to mark sacred times, and days and years, [15] and let them be lights in the vault of the sky to give light on the earth." And it was so. [16] God made two great lights—the greater light to govern the day and the lesser light to govern the night. He also made the stars. [17] God set them in the vault of the sky to give light on the earth, [18] to govern the day and the night, and to separate light from darkness. And God saw that it was good. [19] And there was evening, and there was morning—the fourth day.

And KJV states;

> [14] And God said, Let there be lights in the firmament of the heaven to divide the day from the night; and let them be for signs, and for seasons, and for days, and years: [15] And let them be for lights in the firmament of the heaven to give light upon the earth: and it was so. [16] And God made two great lights; the greater light to rule the day, and the lesser light to rule the night: he made the stars also. [17] And God set them in the firmament of the heaven to give light upon the earth, [18] And to rule over the day and over the night, and to divide the light from the darkness: and God saw that it was good. [19] And the evening and the morning were the fourth day.

These passages emphasize the significance of the Sun and the Moon as celestial bodies created by God to fulfill specific functions in the order of the universe. The Sun is described as the greater light that rules, or governs the day, providing warmth, light, and sustenance for life on Earth.

"For with thee is the fountain of life: in thy light shall we see light". Psalm 36:9

The Moon, referred to as the lesser light, rules or governs the night, illuminating the darkness and providing a sense of rhythm and order to the cycles of nature.

We are going to delve into deeper understanding of these two lights and juxtaposed how these "Two Great Lights" written about in the Beginning, who were created on the fourth day, are in fact the Two Witnesses the Bible prophesied about in Revelation 11. We will learn how these Two Great Lights, commissioned to "rule" and "govern" the day and night, will be used at their appointed time, to not only testify and do ministry, but will do so at the "sacred time", and "as a sign", as written about in Genesis 1:14-19.

These two ministers will "serve" together, in unison and in one accord, for the same purpose. "Let them serve as signs to mark sacred times". We can stop right there, but follow along with me, as we unwrap these beautiful gifts of lights. Scripture has given us clues after clues, line by line, all consistent. It is both amazing and exciting to discover what has been hidden in front of our eyes, all this time. Only to be revealed at the appointed time, and I am honored to be used by Him.

"Make thy face to shine upon thy servant: save me for thy mercies' sake". Psalm 31:16

THE BEGINNING OF THE END

While Genesis deals with the beginning of His Word, let us investigate, the beginning of the end as written about in Revelation 11, 1 -15.

11 *And there was given me a reed like unto a rod: and the angel stood, saying, Rise, and measure the temple of God, and the altar, and them that worship therein.* [2] *But the court which is without the temple leave out, and measure it not; for it is given unto the Gentiles: and the holy city shall they tread under foot forty and two months.* [3] <u>*And I will give power unto my two witnesses,*</u> *and they shall prophesy a thousand two hundred and threescore days, clothed in sackcloth.* [4] *These are the two olive trees, and the two candlesticks standing before the God of the earth.* [5] *And if any man will hurt them, fire proceedeth out of their mouth, and devoureth their enemies: and if any man will hurt them, he must in this manner be killed.* [6] *These have power to shut heaven, that it rain not in the days of their prophecy: and have power over waters to turn them to blood, and to smite the earth with all plagues, as often as they will.* [7] *And when they shall have finished their testimony, the beast that ascendeth out of the bottomless pit shall make war against them, and shall overcome them, and kill them.* [8] *And their dead bodies shall lie in the street of the great city, which spiritually is called Sodom and Egypt, where also our Lord was crucified.* [9] *And they of the people and kindreds and tongues and nations shall see their dead bodies three days and an half, and shall not suffer their dead bodies to be put in graves.* [10] *And they that dwell upon the earth shall rejoice over them, and make merry, and shall send gifts one to another; because these two prophets tormented them that dwelt on the earth.* [11] *And after three days and an half the spirit of life from God entered into them, and they stood upon their feet; and great fear fell upon them which saw them.* [12] *And they heard a great voice from heaven saying unto them, Come up hither. And they ascended up to heaven in a cloud; and their enemies beheld them.* [13] *And the same hour was there a great earthquake, and the tenth part of the city fell, and in the earthquake were slain of men seven thousand: and the remnant were affrighted, and gave glory to the God of heaven.* [14] *The second woe is past; and, behold, the third woe cometh quickly.* [15] *And the seventh angel sounded; and there were great voices in heaven, saying, The kingdoms of this world are become the kingdoms of our Lord, and of his Christ; and he shall reign for ever and ever.*

"But ye are a chosen generation, a royal priesthood, an holy nation, a peculiar people; that ye should shew forth the praises of him who hath called you out of darkness into his marvellous light". 1st Peter 2:9

In the Book of Revelation Chapter 11, the two witnesses are significant. They are representation of the times in the prophetic ministry and witness of God's faithfulness during the end times. The Book itself, "Revelation" is one pertinent clue, that something unknown will be made known.

What no one knows is when these happenings shall occur. The Bible tells us in Matthew 24:36, and again in Mark 13:32 that "no one knows the day or the hour" of the Lord's return. What Revelation has given us, though is the chain of events as to the order of what is to come. Luke outlines in Chapter 24 verses 6-24 in detail what this chain of events will consist of. He tells us when we see these happenings, to "look up because redemption draweth near".

While reading and Purposelypondering on Revelation, I had to stop several times to try to decode and comprehend what I was actually seeing before my eyes. I found myself reading the same verses over and over, again and again, to make sure that what I was seeing with my natural eyes, was actually what was written. It was true. The overwhelming similarities that were glaringly evident, could not be denied. There was just too much evidence, that conferred with the scriptural Two Witnesses that matched the function and characteristics of the Two Witness, as the sun and the moon. Was that because they are one and the same? I couldn't unsee it. But how do I make others see it? I needed to find proof.

"For ye were sometimes darkness, but now are ye light in the Lord: walk as children of light" Ephesians 5:8

★ CHAPTER 2: WHO OR WHAT IS A WITNESS?

Let's start by understanding the term "witness". It's important to note, Scripture never differentiated if these two were male or female, or even human for that matter. The two were only called, "Two Witnesses". In King James, they are referred to as, "These", "They", "Them", in that order. Never as human. The word "Witness", itself can have different meanings depending on the context in which it is used. Let's go a little bit deeper into understanding what a witness is, and what John or better yet, God was saying concerning "Them".

THERE'S ALWAYS A WITNESS?

In a legal context, a witness is a person who has firsthand knowledge of an event or situation and is called upon to testify about what they know in a court of law. The testimony provided by a witness can be used as evidence to help determine the truth of a matter.

In a religious or scriptural context, a witness can refer to someone who testifies to the truth of a belief, a divine revelation, or an event. Witnesses in religious texts may attest to miracles, teachings, or experiences that are considered significant within the faith tradition.

"Ye are the light of the world. A city that is set on an hill cannot be hid". Matthew 5:14

In a broader sense, a witness is someone who sees, hears, or otherwise experiences an event and can provide an account of what occurred. Witnesses play a crucial role in helping to establish the facts of a situation or event.

In a more metaphorical sense, the term "witness" can also refer to any object, document, or other form of evidence that attests to the truth or existence of something. Overall, the concept of a witness involves someone or something that provides testimony, evidence, or support for a particular claim, event, or belief

The Bible contains numerous accounts of individuals who served as witnesses to various events, miracles, and teachings. There are many examples to draw from, some prominent examples of witnesses in the Bible includes various forms of witnesses. This includes Human, Angelic, Inanimate, nature and even the cosmos, all very important.

BIBLICAL WITNESSES: HUMAN AND ANGELIC

The twelve disciples were witnesses to the ministry, teachings, miracles, death, and resurrection of Jesus Christ. They played a crucial role in spreading the message of Christianity after Jesus' ascension. Acts 1:8 (NIV) - "But you will receive power when the Holy Spirit comes on you; and you will be my witnesses in Jerusalem, and in all Judea and Samaria, and to the ends of the earth." Another Biblical witness, was Mary Magdalene. She was a follower of

Jesus and was one of the first witnesses to his resurrection. She is often referred to as the "apostle to the apostles" because she was tasked with telling the disciples that Jesus had risen from the dead.

"When Jesus spoke again to the people, he said, "I am the light of the world. Whoever follows me will never walk in darkness, but will have the light of life." John 8:12

Paul (formerly Saul of Tarsus) was a persecutor of Christians before he encountered the risen Jesus on the road to Damascus. After his conversion, he became a devoted follower of Christ and a key witness to the resurrection.

Stephen, was one of the early Christian martyrs and the first recorded Christian martyr in the Bible. He gave a powerful testimony to the Jewish religious leaders before being stoned to death.

John the Baptist bore witness to Jesus as the Messiah and prepared the way for his ministry. He baptized Jesus and proclaimed him as the Lamb of God.

Anna the Prophetess is a figure mentioned in the Bible who is associated with witnessing Christ. Anna was a prophetess who appears in the Gospel of Luke in the New Testament. She is described as a devout woman who lived in the temple in Jerusalem and worshipped there with fasting and prayer night and day. Anna's encounter with the infant Jesus is recorded in the Gospel of Luke, specifically in Luke 2:36-38 (NIV): *"And there was a prophet, Anna, the daughter of Phanuel, of the tribe of Asher. She was very old; she had lived with her husband seven years after her marriage, and then was a widow until she was eighty-four. She never left the temple but worshiped night and day, fasting and praying. Coming up to them at that very moment, she gave thanks to God and spoke about the child to all who were looking forward to the redemption of Jerusalem."*

"Then I saw that wisdom excelleth folly, as far as light excelleth darkness". Ecclesiastic 2:13

Anna is portrayed as one of the witnesses who recognized the significance of Jesus as the Messiah and spoke about Him to others. Her testimony adds to the growing number of people who bore witness to the identity and mission of Jesus Christ in the early days of His life., and even still today.

Not all witnesses were humans. Angels are spiritual beings who often served as messengers and witnesses in biblical accounts, delivering important messages to individuals such as Mary, Joseph, and the shepherds at the birth of Jesus.

These are just a few examples of witnesses in the Bible.

Throughout both the Old and New Testaments, many individuals played roles as witnesses to God's teachings, actions and power in the lives of people.

Biblical Inanimate Witnesses

While witnesses have been human and celestial beings, there are instances where inanimate objects or elements are described as witnesses to events or covenants. Here are a few examples along with corresponding scriptures:

1. Stones - Joshua 24:27: "And Joshua said to all the people, 'Behold, this stone shall be a witness against us, for it has heard all the words of the Lord that he spoke to us. Therefore, it shall be a witness against you, lest you deal falsely with your God".

"Therefore, whatsoever ye have spoken in darkness shall be heard in the light; and that which ye have spoken in the ear in closets shall be proclaimed upon the housetops". Luke 12: 3

In this verse from the Book of Joshua, Joshua sets up a stone as a witness to the covenant between the Israelites and God. The stone is symbolically portrayed as having heard the words spoken and will serve as a witness against the people if they do not remain faithful to God. 2. Pillar - Laban and Jacob set up a pillar as a witness to their covenant and agreement. Genesis 31:45-52 describes a significant event in the life of Jacob, one of the patriarchs of Israel.

"45 And Jacob took a stone, and set it up for a pillar. 46 And Jacob said unto his brethren, Gather stones; and they took stones, and made an heap: and they did eat there upon the heap. 47 And Laban called it Jegarsahadutha: but Jacob called it Galeed. 48 And Laban said, This heap is a witness between me and thee this day. Therefore was the name of it called Galeed; 49 And Mizpah; for he said, The LORD watch between me and thee, when we are absent one from another.

⁵⁰ If thou shalt afflict my daughters, or if thou shalt take other wives beside my daughters, no man is with us; see, God is witness betwixt me and thee. ⁵¹ And Laban said to Jacob, Behold this heap, and behold this pillar, which I have cast betwixt me and thee: ⁵² This heap be witness, and this pillar be witness, that I will not pass over this heap to thee, and that thou shalt not pass over this heap and this pillar unto me, for harm".

Jacob and Laban decide to set up a witness and a heap of stones as a physical reminder of the covenant they are making.

This was a common practice in ancient times to mark agreements or alliances.

Laban tells Jacob to take an oath in the name of the God of Abraham and the God of Nahor (Laban's father) to not mistreat Laban's daughters or take other wives besides them. Jacob agrees and swears by the Fear of his father Isaac. They then set up a stone pillar and make a meal together to seal the covenant. Laban declares that this heap and pillar will serve as a witness between them and a boundary marker to indicate that they will not cross over to harm each other. Laban promises not to pass the pillar to harm Jacob, and Jacob promises not to pass the pillar to harm Laban. This covenant marked the end of the conflict between Jacob and Laban and established a boundary of peace and respect between them. It was a way to ensure that both parties would honor their agreement and live in harmony despite their past grievances.

" And this is the condemnation, that light is come into the world, and men loved darkness rather than light, because their deeds were evil. ". John 3:19

3. Memorial - Joshua 4:7 "Then you shall answer them that the waters of the Jordan were cut off before the ark of the covenant of the Lord. When it passed over the Jordan, the waters of the Jordan were cut off. So, these stones shall be to the people of Israel a memorial forever."

4. Heaven and Earth -Deuteronomy 30:19: "I call heaven and earth to witness against you today, that I have set before you life and death, blessing and curse. Therefore, choose life, that you and your offspring may live."

5. Altar - Joshua 22:26-27: "Therefore we said, 'Let us now build an altar, not for burnt offering, nor for sacrifice, but to be a witness between us and you, and between our generations after us, that we do perform the service of the Lord in his presence with our burnt offerings and

sacrifices and peace offerings, so your children will not say to our children in time to come, 'You have no portion in the Lord.'"

So, it is very evident that the Lord has used His creation in many instances as we see in the examples given for Biblical witnesses. Other than human forms, celestial beings (angels), and inanimate objects, nature is also used as a witness of God:

"The night is far spent, the day is at hand: let us therefore cast off the works of darkness, and let us put on the armour of light". Romans 13:12

NATURE AS WITNESS

1. Rain - In the King James Version (KJV) of the Bible, Acts 14:17 reads as follows:

"Nevertheless, he left not himself without witness, in that he did good, and gave us rain from heaven, and fruitful seasons, filling our hearts with food and gladness."

In this verse, Paul is emphasizing to the people of Lystra and Derbe that God has not left Himself without a witness or testimony among them.

The witness or testimony of God's existence and goodness is evident in the way He interacts with the world and provides for His creation.

Paul points out that God's witness is displayed through His acts of kindness, such as sending rain from heaven to water the earth and bring forth fruitful seasons. This provision of rain and bountiful harvests demonstrates God's care and providence for His people. As it sustains them by providing food and meeting their physical needs and filling them with joy and gladness.

Overall, Acts 14:17 in the King James Version highlights the idea that God's witness can be seen in the natural world and in the way He blesses and sustains His creation, showcasing His goodness and care for all humanity. It is amazing to see the omniscient, omnipotent, omnipresent character of God as He leaves His mark on Earth before time.

Even His promises and covenants are accompanied by nature confirming what He said.

"The people which sat in darkness saw great light; and to them which sat in the region and shadow of death light is sprung up". Matthew 4:16

2. Rainbow - The rainbow is often seen as a symbol in religious and cultural contexts, including in the Bible.

In the Christian Bible, the rainbow is mentioned in the book of Genesis, specifically in Genesis 9:13-16 (NIV): "I have set my rainbow in the clouds, and it will be the sign of the covenant between me and the earth. Whenever I bring clouds over the earth and the rainbow appears in the clouds, I will remember my covenant between me and you and all living creatures of every kind. Never again will the waters become a flood to destroy all life. Whenever the rainbow appears in the clouds, I will see it and remember the everlasting covenant between God and all living creatures of every kind on the earth." In this passage, the rainbow is described as a sign of God's covenant with humanity, representing a promise of protection and mercy. The rainbow serves as a reminder of this covenant and of God's faithfulness.

These examples illustrate the symbolic use of inanimate objects as witnesses in the Bible to signify important events, covenants, or agreements in the presence of God.

These verses illustrate how people, celestial beings, inanimate objects, and nature can be used symbolically and literally to represent witnesses to agreements, covenant, promises, or events in the presence of God.

"**Let your light so shine before men, that they may see your good works, and glorify your Father which is in heaven**". Matthew 5:16

SIGNIFICANCE, MODEL, AND DESIGN OF WITNESSES

The concept and significance of "biblical witnesses" typically refers to the idea that events or statements in the Bible are confirmed by multiple sources within the text itself. This idea is based on a principle found in the Bible, particularly in the Old Testament, that important matters should be established by the testimony of two or three witnesses.

There is scriptural evidence of this in 2 Corinthians 13. Paul wrote, (**KJV**) "This is the third time I am coming to you. In the mouth of two or three witnesses shall every word be established". It is not coincidence that there are 2 Candlestick and 2 Olive tree, two shall become one. So, one of each is "Two Witnesses". This isn't a fluke, or an oversight, it is the Providential Hand of a Divine Designer. It is by God's design. The Sun and the Moon. Two Olive tree, Two Candlestick/ Lampstand. No mistake there. God is a God of order. Here are models or examples found in scripture regarding numbers of witnesses.

1. Deuteronomy 19:15 (NIV): "One witness is not enough to convict anyone accused of any crime or offense they may have committed. A matter must be established by the testimony of two or three witnesses."

2. Matthew 18:16 (NIV): "But if they will not listen, take one or two others along, so that 'every matter may be established by the testimony of two or three witnesses.'"

3. 2 Corinthians 13:1 (**NIV**): "This will be my third visit to you. 'Every matter must be established by the testimony of two or three witnesses.'"

But he that doeth truth cometh to the light, that his deeds may be made manifest, that they are wrought in God". John 3:21

These verses emphasize the importance of having multiple witnesses to establish the truth of a matter. This principle is meant to ensure fairness and accuracy in legal proceedings and the verification of facts in various situations. Surely God in His infinite wisdom has designed these two luminaries to be hiding in plain sight, waiting for power to be given to them.

We have covered what the definition of a witness is, and who has been used as witness in the Bible, both Old and in New Testament.

We have read where witnesses can be, such as in the sky (in the case of the rainbow), and the multiple ways in how witnesses can be utilized. What we don't know is when these occurrences will take place. Although many have scientifically tried to come up with date or the time frame of when these Two Witnesses will emerge, His word is clear that no one know, or will know when, His appearance will be.

We are certain that He will arrive, however He tell us not to be fooled.

"⁸ He was not that Light, but was sent to bear witness of that Light." John 1:8

★ CHAPTER 3- WHEN SHALL THESE THINGS BE?

"But of that day and that hour knoweth no man, no, not the angels which are in heaven, neither the Son, but the Father". Mark 13:32

It is important to point out that no one knows the very hour that Jesus will return. What we do know is that He will return. We also know the chain of events, according to His Word, that will take place before He puts in His appearance. It is noteworthy to include in this writing what the order of events will be according to His Word.

CHRONONLOGICAL ORDER OF RAPTURE AND TRIBULATION

FIRST, THE RAPTURE- The Rapture is a sudden taking away of Believers. It is of blessed hope that, in the "twinkling of an eye" First the dead in Christ will rise, then those who are alive will be taken away and caught up in the air to meet Jesus. This event happens prior to the Tribulation.

1st Thessalonians 4:16-18 tells us that, "For the Lord himself shall descend from heaven with a shout, with the voice of the archangel, and with the trump of God: and the dead in Christ shall rise first:[17] Then we which are alive and remain shall be caught up together with them in the clouds, to meet the Lord in the air: and so shall we ever be with the Lord.[18] Wherefore comfort one another with these words". Hallelujah!

"Every good gift and every perfect gift is from above, and cometh down from the Father of lights, with whom is no variableness, neither shadow of turning". James 1:17

So, the Rapture will happen FIRST. No one knows when so get ready, get ready, get ready!!! In fact, BE READY so we don't have to try and get ready. Preparation as that of the five wise virgin is the key. Keeping the oil burning in the lamp. Matthew 25:1-13.

"Then shall the kingdom of heaven be likened unto ten virgins, which took their lamps, and went forth to meet the bridegroom. 2 And five of them were wise, and five were foolish. 3 They that were foolish took their lamps, and took no oil with them: 4 But the wise took oil in their vessels with their lamps. 5 While the bridegroom tarried, they all slumbered and slept. 6 And at midnight there was a cry made, Behold, the bridegroom cometh; go ye out to meet him. 7 Then all those virgins arose, and trimmed their lamps. 8 And the foolish said unto the wise, Give us of your oil; for our lamps are gone out. 9 But the wise answered, saying, Not so; lest there be not enough for us and you: but go ye rather to them that sell, and buy for yourselves. 10 And while they went to buy, the bridegroom came; and they that were ready went in with him to the marriage: and the door was shut. 11 Afterward came also the other virgins, saying, Lord, Lord, open to us. 12 But he answered and said, Verily I say unto you, I know you not. 13 Watch therefore, for ye know neither the day nor the hour wherein the Son of man cometh".

AFTER THE RAPTURE, THEN THE TRIBULATION - The Tribulation is the period immediately following the rapture. This time period, the Bible tells us, is a time of intense tribulation all over Earth.

5 "As long as I am in the world, I am the light of the world". John 9:5

This tribulation lasts for seven years and includes trials and judgement. The seven year is broken up in the first 3 and a half, and the second 3 and a half is deemed to be considered the Great Tribulation period.

This is the period that Revelation 6 to Revelation 18 covers. This is the time period in which the Two Witnesses begin their prophetic assignment.

This is also the time period in which the Beast is identified. It is during this time the Antichrist rises to power. This writer has already shared that the Antichrist is, systems, laws, practices and order, that are against Christ. The Beast is discussed more in Chapter 13, titled, The Beast.

So those who become Christians on Earth at this time period, who do not take the vaccine, will be easily detected. Christians will be under heavy judgement and extreme persecution, and torture.

Hence the "Great" Tribulation. "For then shall be great tribulation, such as was not since the beginning of the world to this time, no, nor ever shall be". Matthew 24:21.

"The light of the body is the eye: therefore when thine eye is single, thy whole body also is full of light; but when thine eye is evil, thy body also is full of darkness". Luke 11:34

As horrible as this time period is, due to the extreme torture of the people. There will be some that recognize that Jesus is Christ, and repent. Of those that repent, some will be tortured, and choose martyrdom by deciding to die for Christ. The Bible depicts that, this is the time period, known as "Jacob's trouble"

JACOB'S TROUBLE

Jacob's Trouble or Jacob's distress, refers to the nation of Israel that has denied Christ. They will experience persecution and natural disaster, however "he shall be saved out of it.

> [7] Alas! for that day is great, so that none is like it: it is even the time of Jacob's trouble, but he shall be saved out of it. [8] For it shall come to pass in that day, saith the LORD of hosts, that I will break his yoke from off thy neck, and will burst thy bonds, and strangers shall no more serve themselves of him: [9] But they shall serve the LORD their God, and David their king, whom I will raise up unto them. [10] Therefore fear thou not, O my servant Jacob, saith the LORD; neither be dismayed, O Israel: for, lo, I will save thee from afar, and thy seed from the land of their captivity; and Jacob shall return, and shall be in rest, and be quiet, and none shall make him afraid. [11] For I am with thee, saith the LORD, to save thee: though I make a full end of all nations whither I have scattered thee, yet I will not make a full end of thee: but I will correct thee in measure, and will not leave thee altogether unpunished. [12] For thus saith the LORD, Thy bruise is incurable, and thy wound is grievous. [13] There is none to plead thy cause, that thou mayest be bound up: thou hast no healing medicines. [14] All thy lovers have forgotten thee; they seek thee not; for I have wounded thee with the wound of an enemy, with the chastisement of a cruel one, for the multitude of thine iniquity;

because thy sins were increased.¹⁵ Why criest thou for thine affliction? thy sorrow is incurable for the multitude of thine iniquity: because thy sins were increased, I have done these things unto thee.¹⁶ Therefore all they that devour thee shall be devoured; and all thine adversaries, every one of them, shall go into captivity; and they that spoil thee shall be a spoil, and all that prey upon thee will I give for a prey.¹⁷ For I will restore health unto thee, and I will heal thee of thy wounds, saith the LORD; because they called thee an Outcast, saying, This is Zion, whom no man seeketh after.¹⁸ Thus saith the LORD; Behold, I will bring again the captivity of Jacob's tents, and have mercy on his dwellingplaces; and the city shall be

"Neither do men light a candle, and put it under a bushel, but on a candlestick; and it giveth light unto all that are in the house". Matthew 5: 15

builded upon her own heap, and the palace shall remain after the manner thereof.¹⁹ And out of them shall proceed thanksgiving and the voice of them that make merry: and I will multiply them, and they shall not be few; I will also glorify them, and they shall not be small.²⁰ Their children also shall be as aforetime, and their congregation shall be established before me, and I will punish all that oppress them.²¹ And their nobles shall be of themselves, and their governor shall proceed from the midst of them; and I will cause him to draw near, and he shall approach unto me: for who is this that engaged his heart to approach unto me? saith the LORD.²² And ye shall be my people, and I will be your God.²³ Behold, the whirlwind of the LORD goeth forth with fury, a continuing whirlwind: it shall fall with pain upon the head of the wicked.²⁴ The fierce anger of the LORD shall not return, until he hath done it, and until he have performed the intents of his heart: in the latter days ye shall consider it.

ENGRAFTING AND INGATHERING

God is so good. It's not just a saying He is perfect, divine, and in order.

Is it a coincidence that Apostle Paul uses the analogy of an olive tree in Romans 11 to illustrate God's children being engrafted, or ingrafted in as God's covenant people? Meanwhile Revelation 11 speak of that time using the same analogy of the Olive tree, with the nation of Israel. Is that coincidental that the olive tree is a representative of both the Jews and the Gentiles, and that the two olive trees is made mention symbolically? I think not! Glory to God! Grafting is a technique used in horticulture, to join two plants together using their tissue. In essence you use a bud or what is called a <u>scion</u>, and you position it in a way that would joins the stem from another plant, and they join together, form a stock, and continue to grow as one.

"For so hath the Lord commanded us, saying, I have set thee to be a light of the Gentiles, that thou shouldest be for salvation unto the ends of the earth". Acts 13:47

Engrafting signifies the spiritual union and incorporation of Gentile believers into the heritage and promises of God's covenant people, symbolized by Israel. The apostle Paul uses the analogy of an olive tree in Romans 11 to illustrate this idea. In this metaphor, the cultivated olive tree represents the people of God, while the wild olive branches represent Gentile believers. Through faith in Jesus Christ, Gentile believers are spiritually grafted into the olive tree, sharing in the blessings, spiritually benefitting and receiving the promises of God's covenant with Israel.

Romans 11: 15-26

"[15] For if the casting away of them be the reconciling of the world, what shall the receiving of them be, but life from the dead? [16] For if the firstfruit be holy, the lump is also holy: and if the root be holy, so are the branches. [17] And if some of the branches be broken off, and thou, being a wild olive tree, wert grafted in among them, and with them partakest of the root and fatness of the olive tree; [18] Boast not against the branches. But if thou boast, thou bearest not the root, but the root thee. [19] Thou wilt say then, The branches were broken off, that I might be grafted in. [20] Well; because of unbelief they were broken off, and thou standest by faith. Be not highminded, but fear: [21] For if God spared not the natural branches, take heed lest he also spare not thee. [22] Behold therefore the goodness and severity of God: on them which fell, severity; but toward thee, goodness, if thou continue in his goodness: otherwise thou also shalt be cut off. [23] And they also, if they abide not still in unbelief, shall be grafted in: for God is able to graft them in again. [24] For if thou wert cut out of the olive tree which is wild by nature, and wert grafted contrary to nature into a good olive tree: how much more shall these, which be the natural branches, be grafted into their own olive tree? [25] For I would not, brethren, that ye should be ignorant of this mystery, lest ye should be wise in your own conceits; that blindness in part is happened to Israel, until the fulness of the Gentiles be come in. [26] And so all Israel shall be saved: as it is written, there shall come out of Sion the Deliverer, and shall turn away ungodliness from Jacob.

"Arise, shine; for thy light is come, and the glory of the Lord is risen upon thee". Isaiah 60:1

Is that why Revelation 11:1-2 specifies not to measure the outer courts that was given to the Gentiles? Does this mean that it was now time for the ingathering of another harvest?

"I was given a reed like a measuring rod and was told, "Go and measure the temple of God and the altar, with its worshipers. ²But exclude the outer court; do not measure it, because it has been given to the Gentiles. They will trample on the holy city for 42 months".

Let's look more into this.

Ingathering refers to the gathering together of people from all nations, including Jews and Gentiles, into the community of believers under Christ. It reflects the universal scope of God's redemptive plan, where people from diverse backgrounds are welcomed into the family of God through faith in Jesus Christ. The concept of ingathering highlights the inclusive nature of God's salvation, where all are invited to partake in the blessings of the kingdom of God, regardless of their ethnic or cultural backgrounds.

These concepts emphasize the unity, reconciliation, and mutual participation of believers from different backgrounds within the body of Christ. Through engrafting and ingathering, believers are united in Christ, sharing in the inheritance and promises of God's kingdom. The New Testament teaches that in Christ, there is no distinction between Jew and Gentile, but all are one in Him, forming a new spiritual family that transcends human divisions and unites believers in love, faith, and fellowship.

"That Christ should suffer, and that he should be the first that should rise from the dead, and should shew light unto the people, and to the Gentiles". Acts 22:23

The engrafting and ingathering of Jews and Gentiles reflect the transformative power of the gospel to bring together people from diverse backgrounds into a unified community of faith, demonstrating the richness and diversity of God's kingdom on earth.

"The eyes of your understanding being enlightened; that ye may know what is the hope of his calling, and what the riches of the glory of his inheritance in the saints" Ephesians 1:18

⭐ CHAPTER 4: SIGNS SHALL FOLLOW THE BELIEVER

The signs that are said to foretell the second coming of Christ are a significant topic in Christian theology and eschatology today. While the rapture will be a suddenly, this will immediately alert those left behind that know of Christ to definitely start paying attention, and to accept Him as their savior. Let's look into some Biblical examples as to what was prophesied in the Old and New Testament, prophesied by Jesus, and some other interesting notable signs that confirms that signs shall follow the believer.

There are many signs. These texts are often interpreted from various passages, including the New Testament, and the Old Testament.

COMMONLY EXPECTED SIGNS

Here are some of the signs that are commonly believed to signal the second coming, along with references to scientific and historical perspectives:

1. *Biblical Signs

Wars and rumors of wars: In Matthew 24:6-7, Jesus speaks of wars and rumors of wars as signs of the end times.

  - Natural disasters In Matthew 24:7 and Revelation 6:12-14, earthquakes, famines, and other natural disasters are mentioned as signs.

  - The rise of false prophets and false Christs Matthew 24:11 warns of false prophets and false messiahs who will deceive many.

"Ye are all the children of light, and the children of the day: we are not of the night, nor of darkness". 1 Thessalonians 5:5

- Persecution of believers: In Matthew 24:9-10, Jesus speaks of persecution of believers in the end times.

- The gospel being preached to all nations: In Matthew 24:14, Jesus states that the gospel will be preached to all nations before the end comes.

OTHER SIGNS

2. Scientific Signs:

- Some people interpret signs such as climate change, environmental degradation, and technological advancements as modern-day indicators that align with the biblical prophecies of natural disasters and the increase of knowledge (Daniel 12:4).

- Scientific advancements that could potentially lead to global crises or conflicts, such as advancements in weapons technology or bioengineering, are sometimes seen as signs of the end times.

3. Historical Signs:

- Throughout history, there have been periods of intense conflict, war, and persecution that some have interpreted as signs of the end times,

- The formation of the nation of Israel in 1948 is often seen as a significant event in relation to end-time prophecies, particularly those concerning the restoration of Israel.

- The spread of Christianity to the Four Corners of the world, and the increased interconnectedness of the world through technology and globalization are also seen by some as fulfilling biblical prophecies regarding the preaching of the gospel to all nations.

"And he said, It is a light thing that thou shouldest be my servant to raise up the tribes of Jacob, and to restore the preserved of Israel: I will also give thee for a light to the Gentiles, that thou mayest be my salvation unto the end of the earth". Isaiah 49:6

4. Cosmic Signs and Disturbances -In the Bible, there are several references to the sky being dark or celestial disturbances occurring in the context of tribulation. Here are some examples: ALL of that to say, Jesus mentioned that there will be signs that will be

seen in the sun, moon, and stars. Jesus specified what will precede His second coming and the end times. Let's look a little bit deeper into His discourse.

THE OLIVET DISCOURSE

The discourse is a teaching given by Jesus to his disciples on the Mount of Olives (also known as the Mount Olives or Mount Olivet) regarding future events, the end times, and the second coming of Christ. Here are some key scriptures that form the basis of what theologians coined, the "Olivet Discourse". The Olivet Discourse is primarily based

on passages found in the Synoptic Gospels of Matthew, Mark, and Luke. Matthew 24:1-51**: This chapter in the Gospel of Matthew contains a detailed account of Jesus' teachings about the signs of the end times, the coming of the Son of Man, and the need for readiness and vigilance. It includes prophecies about wars, famines, earthquakes, false prophets, and the abomination of desolation. **Luke 21:5-36**:

"No man, when he hath lighted a candle, putteth it in a secret place, neither under a bushel, but on a candlestick, that they which come in may see the light". Luke 11:33

The Olivet Discourse in the Gospel of Luke contains similar themes to Matthew and Mark, including prophecies about the destruction of the Temple, signs preceding the end times, and the coming of the Son of Man. Jesus also emphasizes the need for perseverance and prayer. **Mark 13:1-37**: Mark's account of the Olivet Discourse parallels much of what is found in Matthew 24. It also includes Jesus' warnings about deception, persecution, the coming of the Son of Man, and the need to be watchful These passages are foundational and provide the basis for eschatology and the study of end times theology. They have been the subject of much interpretation and debate among theologians, scholars, and believers throughout history.

NEW AND OLD TESTAMENT ACCOUNT OF SIGNS

1.   Luke   21:25-26

"There will be signs in the sun, moon and stars. On the earth, nations will be in anguish and perplexity at the roaring and tossing of the sea.

26 People will faint from terror, apprehensive of what is coming on the world, for the heavenly bodies will be shaken."

"For they got not the land in possession by their own sword, neither did their own arm save them: but thy right hand, and thine arm, and the light of thy countenance, because thou hadst a favour unto them". Psalm 44:3

2.. Mark 13:24-26:
"But in those days, after that tribulation, the sun will be darkened, and the moon will not give its light, and the stars will be falling from heaven, and the powers in the heavens will be shaken. And then they will see the Son of Man coming in clouds with great power and glory."

3. Joel 2:31: "The sun shall be turned into darkness, and the moon into blood, before the great and awesome day of the Lord comes."

4. Ezekiel 32:7-8 (Old Testament - Book of Ezekiel): "And when I blot you out, I will cover the heavens and make their stars dark; I will cover the sun with a cloud, and the moon shall not give its

light. All the bright lights of heaven will I make dark over you, and put darkness on your land, declares the Lord God."

(In this passage, Ezekiel prophesies against Egypt using imagery of cosmic darkness and the darkening of celestial bodies as a sign of judgment and destruction that will come upon the nation).

.5. Isaiah (Old Testament - Book of Isaiah mentions twice. First in Isaiah 13:10-11 and then later in 50:3) "The stars of heaven and their constellations will not show their light. The rising sun will be darkened and the moon will not give its light. 11 I will punish the world for its evil, the wicked for their sins".

"In him was life; and the life was the light of men". John 1:4

50:3 "I clothe the heavens with blackness and make sackcloth their covering." (This verse from Isaiah uses poetic language to describe God's power and sovereignty over creation. The imagery of blackening the heavens and covering them with sackcloth conveys a sense of mourning and judgment, emphasizing God's authority over all things). We will discuss "Sackcloth" more in details in chapter 5 titled, "Dressed for the Occasion; Sackcloth".

6. Matthew 24:29: "Immediately after the tribulation of those days the sun will be darkened, and the moon will not give its light, and the stars will fall from heaven, and the powers of the heavens will be shaken." This passage in the New Testament, spoken by Jesus in the Olivet Discourse, describes celestial disturbances that will occur after a period of tribulation.

These passages from Joel, Luke, Mark, Ezekiel, Isaiah and Matthew all illustrates how the Bible uses celestial references and cosmic phenomena when explaining divine judgment, tribulation, and significant events in the context of prophecy and eschatology.

FOUR HIS GLORY

Speaking of signs, one very undeniably noticeable commonality, (I don't believe this is coincidence, however not saying this is prophecy) was the common reoccurrence of the number 4. This writer noticed during this writing, there was a consistence significance with the number four. In religious and spiritual contexts, the number four often carries symbolic significance such as completion, or edification. Let's explore the significance of the fourth day of creation and the concept of the fourth angel

"If I rise on the wings of the dawn, if I settle on the far side of the sea, 10 even there your hand will guide me, your right hand will hold me fast. 11 If I say, "Surely the darkness will hide me and the light become night around me," Psalm 139: 9-11

1. Fourth Day of Creation (Genesis 1:14-19):

In the biblical creation account in the Book of Genesis, the fourth day is significant because it is when God created the Sun, Moon, and stars. These celestial bodies were created to govern the day and night, provide light, mark time, and serve as signs for seasons, days, and years. The creation of the Sun and the Moon on the fourth day symbolizes God's order, power, and provision in establishing the natural cycles of the universe.

2. Fourth Angel:

The concept of the "fourth angel" is often associated with the Book of Revelation in the New Testament. In Revelation 8:12, it mentions the fourth angel sounding a trumpet, signaling catastrophic events that will occur during the end times. The blowing of the trumpets by the seven angels is said to herald significant events leading up to the final judgment and the establishment of God's kingdom.

Revelation 8:12 (NIV)

"The fourth angel sounded his trumpet, and a third of the sun was struck, a third of the moon, and a third of the stars, so that a third of them turned dark. A third of the day was without light, and also a third of the night." Overall, the number four is often seen as symbolizing stability, completion, and earthly manifestations in various religious and spiritual contexts.

"Then Jesus said unto them, Yet a little while is the light with you. Walk while ye have the light, lest darkness come upon you: for he that walketh in darkness knoweth not whither he goeth". John 12:35

The fourth day of creation and the concept of the fourth angel carry symbolic meanings that convey themes of order, divine intervention, and the unfolding of God's plan in the universe. In the Book of Revelation, the fourth angel is one of the seven angels who are described as sounding trumpets to announce various events related to the end times and the judgment of God.

The sounding of the seven trumpets is a series of cataclysmic events that are depicted as part of the apocalyptic vision revealed to the apostle John on the island of Patmos. Revelation 16:8-11: In the context of the seven bowl judgments, the fourth angel pours out his bowl on the sun, causing it to scorch people with fire. Despite the intense heat, people do not repent of their sins but instead blaspheme God, highlighting their refusal to acknowledge the need for repentance and mourning. Is it coincidence that the sun, and moon were created on the fourth day, and that it was the fourth angel that "sounded his trumpet, and a third of the sun was struck, a third of the moon, and a third of the stars, so that a third of them turned dark. A third of the day was without light, and also a third of the night"? While I don't believe it was coincidence, it is very interesting to say the very least.

"Then shall thy light break forth as the morning, and thine health shall spring forth speedily: and thy righteousness shall go before thee; the glory of the Lord shall be thy reward". Isaiah 58:8

★ CHAPTER 5-DRESSED FOR THE OCCASION; SACKCLOTH

Now about sackcloth. Defined as a coarse and often dark-colored fabric traditionally woven from goat's hair or other rough materials, sackcloth has been utilized as a tangible symbol of mourning, penitence, and humility throughout history. Sackcloth continues to resonate across cultures and time periods, as a material manifestation of one who is grieving. Embodying the enduring power of symbolism in the human experience.

The act of wearing sackcloth is deeply ingrained in rituals and customs associated with expressions of grief, repentance, and profound sorrow.

DESIGNED BY THE MASTER -WEAR; REVIEWS

In scholarly and historical contexts, sackcloth is typically defined as a course, dark-colored fabric woven from goat's hair or other rough materials, commonly worn as a symbol of mourning, penitence, or humility. It is often associated with expressions of

grief, repentance, or deep sorrow in various religious and cultural traditions.

In the book "The Bible and the Narrative Tradition" by Frank McConnell, the author discusses the symbolic significance of sackcloth in the Bible, particularly in the context of mourning and repentance. McConnell explains how sackcloth was worn by individuals as a sign of humility and a plea for forgiveness in ancient times.

"For thou wilt light my candle: the Lord my God will enlighten my darkness". Psalm 18:28

In an article titled "Sackcloth and Ashes: The Archaeology of Mourning in the Iron Age Levant" by Rachel Hallote, the author explores archaeological evidence of sackcloth and ashes as mourning practices in the ancient Levant region. The article delves into the material culture associated with mourning rituals and the significance of sackcloth in expressing grief and loss. Sackcloth, a term rooted in historical and cultural practices, holds symbolic significance across different societies and religious traditions. Scholars and researchers have delved into the multifaceted meanings and implications of sackcloth in various contexts.

In the realm of biblical studies, sackcloth is often discussed as a visual representation of humility and a plea for forgiveness. The wearing of sackcloth in ancient times signified a profound sense of mourning and a desire for reconciliation with the divine. References to sackcloth in religious texts and historical accounts underscore its role as a visible marker of contrition and submission before higher powers.

Archaeological studies have unearthed evidence of sackcloth and ashes being used in mourning practices in different regions and time periods. By examining archaeological findings and material culture, researchers have gained insights into how sackcloth was woven into the fabric of mourning rituals, serving as a tangible link between the living and the departed. The presence of sackcloth in archaeological contexts speaks to its enduring significance as a ritualistic garment associated with expressions of loss and remembrance.

"22 For there is nothing hid, which shall not be manifested; neither was any thing kept secret, but that it should come abroad". Mark 4:22

In the study of ancient Mesopotamian and Levantine cultures, the significance of wearing sackcloth is done in the context of seeking forgiveness and divine mercy. Furthermore, sackcloth is analyzed as part of penitential rites and religious ceremonies. As scholars explore the cultural and religious practices of these ancient civilizations, they uncover the ways in which sackcloth was employed as a symbol of repentance and atonement. The donning of sackcloth in these contexts reflected a profound spiritual yearning for forgiveness and reconciliation, underscoring the deep-rooted symbolism of this humble fabric. In a religious studies journal article titled "Sackcloth and Ashes: A Study of Penitential Rites in Ancient Mesopotamia" by John Smith, the author examines the use of sackcloth as a symbol of penance and atonement in ancient Mesopotamian religious practices.

These examples illustrate how scholars have defined and described sackcloth in various academic works, highlighting its symbolic and cultural significance in different historical and religious contexts.

Scholars from various disciplines have illuminated the rich tapestry of meanings woven into the fabric of sackcloth. From biblical narratives to archaeological discoveries and historical accounts, the wearing of sackcloth emerges as a poignant symbol of human emotion and spiritual expression.

And I will bring the blind by a way that they knew not; I will lead them in paths that they have not known: I will make darkness light before them, and crooked things straight. These things will I do unto them, and not forsake them". Isaiah 42:16

UNIFORMED FOR DUTY- READY FOR WORK

Ascribing Power "Given" to the Two Witnesses wearing sackcloth denotes, an appointed time of service, and a time of mourning. The giving of power to the Two Witnesses in Revelation signifies their divine commission to serve as instruments of God's will, to testify to His truth. We have already uncovered in the Chapter "What is a Witness", that God in His infinite wisdom, has used His creation as Witnesses, that are able to testify of His goodness, promises, and time of events, by their behavior. Understanding this, and believing His word is important in recognizing and seeing how these things can be. Faith plays a pivotal role in recognizing the unfolding of prophetic events during the end times. "These two", the Sun and the Moon, their empowerment will testify to the sovereignty and authority of God as they carry out their mission amidst challenges and opposition that will be present in these times, hence the symbolism of dressing them in figurative sackcloth. In the Book of Revelation, the giving of power to the Two Witnesses is described in Revelation 11:3-6. The passage explains the empowerment of the Two Witnesses and details the nature of their ministry during a time of tribulation. Here is a brief explanation of when and how power was given to the Two Witnesses as outlined in Revelation.

"And was transfigured before them: and his face did shine as the sun, and his raiment was white as the light". Matthew 17:2

ROLES AND JOB RESPONSIBILITIES

1. When: The power was given to the Two Witnesses at the beginning of their prophetic ministry. In Revelation 11:3, it mentions that God says, "<u>I will give power</u> unto my two witnesses." This indicates that the empowerment of the Two Witnesses occurred at the initiation of their mission to prophesy and testify.

2. Empowerment: The passage describes the specific powers granted to the Two Witnesses by God.

They are endowed with the ability to prophesy for a specified period (1,260 days), symbolizing a time of significant importance.

Additionally, they are given the authority to perform miraculous signs, including the ability to call down fire to consume their enemies, to influence the weather by shutting the heavens so that it does not rain, and to bring plagues upon the earth as a demonstration of God's judgment.

They were given power at this time, however power to do what? Let's look closer. The sun and the moon were given power to:

1. Power to Prophesy: The two witnesses are given the ability to prophesy for 1,260 days, which is symbolic of a specific period of time during which they will bear witness to God's truth and proclaim His message. Sometimes events speak louder than words. For example, the Total Solar Eclipse on Monday April 8th 2024. Not only was it the only thing mentioned on social media, but the feedback and the emotional reaction was extremely telling of the mighty works of God. Some took time out from work to witness, others watched on television, but it was quite a conversation piece.

This writer observed just how much the sun and the moon was testifying of God's goodness, and knew that this was a kairos moment. That was my release to go and write what was shown to me.

"And God said, Let there be light: and there was light". Genesis 1 :3

2. Power of Protection: These two have been given authority to carry out their ministry without being harmed. No harm can come to them, or as the word declares, the same would be done unto them.

3. Power of Judgment: The two witnesses are granted the power to call down fire from their mouths to consume their enemies. This act of judgment symbolizes God's wrath against those who seek to harm or oppose the witnesses. Our Master Planner has designed it, so that if anyone tries to harm these two, they will be hurt.

4. Power over Nature: The two witnesses have the ability to shut the heavens so that it does not rain during the time of their prophesying.

This power over nature mirrors the actions of Old Testament prophets like Elijah, who also had the authority to control the weather as a sign of God's judgment or blessing.

5. Power to Bring Plagues: The passage states that the two witnesses have the authority to strike the earth with various plagues as often as they will. This power to bring plagues serves as a demonstration of God's sovereignty over creation and His ability to execute judgment on the earth.

3. Purpose: The empowerment of the Two Witnesses serves a specific purpose within the context of the events described in Revelation. They are tasked with bearing witness to God's truth, proclaiming His judgment and mercy, and demonstrating His authority over creation during a tumultuous period leading up to the final judgment.

"Do all things without murmurings and disputings: [15] That ye may be blameless and harmless, the sons of God, without rebuke, in the midst of a crooked and perverse nation, among whom ye shine as lights in the world". Phillipians 2:14-15

⭐ CHAPTER 6 - SHUT IT DOWN; GOD IS TALKING

Let's Purposely Ponder for a moment... Has there ever been a time when God manipulated the Sun, the Moon, and just shut down the heavens for His purpose? The scripture says YES! The Old Testament has some fiery examples of when the heavens were manipulated, in order for God to get the glory. Afterall, the Master Artisian IS THE Master Designer.

KING HEZEKIAH AND THE SUNDIAL

King Hezekiah of Judah was seriously ill and prayed to God for healing. He asked the prophet Isaiah for a sign from the Lord that he would be healed and be able to go up to the temple of the Lord on the third day. Isaiah, the prophet, responded with a question to Hezekiah, presenting him with a choice for the sign: whether the shadow on the sundial would go forward ten steps or go back ten steps. - Hezekiah chose the more miraculous option of having the shadow go back ten steps, contrary to the natural movement of shadows. Isaiah then prayed to the Lord, and miraculously, the Lord made the shadow on the sundial go back the ten steps it had previously gone down, as a sign to Hezekiah of God's promise and power to heal him and extend his life.

"If we say that we have fellowship with him, and walk in darkness, we lie, and do not the truth". 1 John 1:6

2 Kings 20:8-11 (NIV):

"8 Hezekiah had asked Isaiah, 'What will be the sign that the Lord will heal me and that I will go up to the temple of the Lord on the third day from now? 9 Isaiah answered, 'This is the Lord's sign to you that the Lord will do what he has promised: Shall the shadow go forward ten steps, or shall it go back ten steps?' 10 'It is a simple matter for the shadow to go forward ten steps,' said Hezekiah. 'Rather, have it go back ten steps.' 11 Then the prophet Isaiah called on the Lord, and the Lord made the shadow go back the ten steps it had gone down on the stairway of Ahaz."

This passage illustrates a miraculous event where God intervened in the natural order by manipulating the movement of the shadow on the sundial as a sign to King Hezekiah. It serves as a demonstration of God's power, and His ability to perform signs and wonders. Hallelujah!

These verses show how there once was signs and will be cosmic disturbances, as signs in the sun, moon, and stars, causing fear and distress among nations. The mention of the sea roaring and tossing can be interpreted as natural disasters and upheavals that will occur as part of the end-time events. The shaking of the heavenly bodies describes the actual upheaval and which results in actual disruption of the natural order as a prelude to the return of Jesus Christ and the final judgment. It's in His word.

"He revealeth the deep and secret things: he knoweth what is in the darkness, and the light dwelleth with him". Daniel 2:22

JOSHUA'S PRAYER STOPPED THE SUN AND THE MOON

Another example of God using His power and affected his creation to obey Him is found with Joshua. I think it's important to know, this isn't the first time that the Sun and the Moon operated outside of their normal functionality. One example of the sun and moon operating outside of their normal function can be found in Joshua 10:12-14 in the Old Testament. This passage describes an event during the conquest of

Canaan when Joshua and the Israelites were fighting against the Amorite kings.

Joshua 10:12-14 (NIV):

"On the day the Lord gave the Amorites over to Israel, Joshua said to the Lord in the presence of Israel: 'Sun, stand still over Gibeon, and you, moon, over the Valley of Aijalon.' So, the sun stood still, and the moon stopped, till the nation avenged itself on its enemies, as it is written in the Book of Jashar. The sun stopped in the middle of the sky and delayed going down about a full day. There has never been a day like it before or since, a day when the Lord listened to a human being. Surely the Lord was fighting for Israel!"

In this passage, Joshua, in the midst of battle, prays for the sun to stand still, and God grants his request. The sun stops in the middle of the sky, extending daylight for a full day, allowing the Israelites to continue their battle against the Amorites and achieve victory. Hallelujah!

"Light is sown for the righteous, and gladness for the upright in heart". Psalm 97:11

6 "They have power to shut up the heavens so that it will not rain during the time they are prophesying; and they have power to turn the waters into blood and to strike the earth with every kind of plague as often as they want".

Many scholars and theologians interpret the passage in Joshua 10 as a poetic or symbolic description of a miraculous event rather than a literal astronomical phenomenon.

Some suggest that it may have been a localized event such as an extended period of daylight rather than a literal stopping of the sun's movement.

Ultimately, the event described in Joshua 10 is a matter of faith and interpretation, and it is open to different understandings based on one's religious beliefs and perspective on the relationship between scripture and science

- The two witnesses are given additional supernatural powers, such as the ability to control the weather (shutting up the heavens so that it does not rain) and to perform various plagues on the earth. These powers demonstrate their authority and divine mandate.

REVELATORY LIGHTS

Specifically In the Book of Revelation, there are passages that describe cosmic signs and events related to the sun and moon. These writings echo what prophets have all seen, and what Jesus has spoken directly.

"Be ye not unequally yoked together with unbelievers: for what fellowship hath righteousness with unrighteousness? and what communion hath light with darkness"? 2nd Corinthians 6:14

This key verse speaks not only of sackcloth, but speaks of activities in the sky, activities that directly mention the sun and moon in the context of apocalyptic events:
1 Revelation 6:12-14 (NIV)
"I watched as he opened the sixth seal. There was a great earthquake.

The sun turned black like sackcloth made of goat hair, the whole moon turned blood red, 13 and the stars in the sky fell to earth, as figs drop from a fig tree when shaken by a strong wind.

14 The heavens receded like a scroll being rolled up, and every mountain and island was removed from its place."

The Book of Revelation depict dramatic cosmic events involving the sun, moon, and stars as part of the apocalyptic visions of John. These cosmic disturbances are an expression of God's judgment and the coming of the end times, signaling significant changes and upheavals in the natural order of the world. The Holy Scripture has consistently repeated this.

THE HEAVENS ARE TALKING- SPEAK GOD

In the Bible, there are references to darkening of the sun, which some interpret as a possible solar eclipse. This event is associated with judgment, the end times, or important historical events.

"Who only hath immortality, dwelling in the light which no man can approach unto; whom no man hath seen, nor can see: to whom be honour and power everlasting. Amen".
1 Timothy 6:16

Here are some instances in the Bible where the darkening of the sun is mentioned:

1. **Crucifixion of Jesus Christ:**

- In the New Testament, the crucifixion of Jesus Christ is accompanied by darkness covering the land. This event is described in the following verses:

- Matthew 27:45 (KJV): "Now from the sixth hour there was darkness over all the land unto the ninth hour."

- Mark 15:33 (KJV): "And when the sixth hour was come, there was darkness over the whole land until the ninth hour."

- Luke 23:44-45 (KJV): "And it was about the sixth hour, and there was a darkness over all the earth until the ninth hour.

This darkness at the crucifixion is often interpreted as a supernatural phenomenon related to the death of Jesus. However, from a scientific perspective, there are a few theories that attempt to explain this event without invoking supernatural causes:

1. Solar Eclipse: Some scholars propose that the darkness at the crucifixion could have been caused by a solar eclipse. While a solar eclipse occurs when the moon passes between the Earth and the sun, causing a temporary shadow on the Earth, a total solar eclipse cannot last for three hours, as described in the Bible. However, it is possible that an unusual type of eclipse or atmospheric conditions could have contributed to a prolonged period of darkness.

"I the Lord have called thee in righteousness, and will hold thine hand, and will keep thee, and give thee for a covenant of the people, for a light of the Gentiles"; Isaiah 42:6

2. Atmospheric Phenomenon: Another theory suggests that the darkness could have been caused by unusual atmospheric conditions, such as a thick layer of clouds or dust in the atmosphere. These conditions could have obscured the sun, leading to a period of darkness during the crucifixion.

3. Volcanic Activity: Some researchers propose that a volcanic eruption could have contributed to the darkness at the crucifixion. Volcanic

eruptions can release ash and particles into the atmosphere, which can block sunlight and lead to a darkened sky.

It is important to note that these scientific explanations are speculative and cannot be definitively proven. The darkness at the crucifixion remains a mysterious event described in the Bible, and interpretations of its cause vary among scholars and theologians.

2. End times prophecy

- The darkening of the sun is also mentioned in Revelation 6:12-13 (KJV): "And I beheld when he had opened the sixth seal, and, lo, there was a great earthquake; and the sun became black as sackcloth of hair, and the moon became as blood; And the

stars of heaven fell unto the earth, even as a fig tree casteth her untimely figs, when she is shaken of a mighty wind." These are just a few examples of instances in the Bible where the darkening of the sun is mentioned. It is often seen as a powerful and symbolic event signifying significant spiritual or historical occurrences. The heavens declare His majesty.

"No man, when he hath lighted a candle, covereth it with a vessel, or putteth it under a bed; but setteth it on a candlestick, that they which enter in may see the light". Luke 8:16

⭐ CHAPTER 7 MR.SUN AND MRS.MOON

No, this isn't worshipping of the sun and the moon. Although doing research for this book this writer learned that there are religions that actually worships the sun and the moon, giving the sun male personality and the moon, it's female counterpart, identity. Let's be very clear here, that isn't what this is! This is where we will delve deeper into symbolism, and compare the evident usage. Grab your creative lens for this one!

HUMAN ATTRIBUTES

Where in the scriptures has the Sun and the Moon symbolically described humans? In both the Bible and the Torah, there are instances where the sun and moon are described using human attributes Let's look at how scripture has given the sun and the moon human personalities and human characteristics using symbolism. One example can be found In Psalm 19:1-6 (NIV), "The heavens declare the glory of God; the skies proclaim the work of his hands.

Day after day they pour forth speech; night after night they reveal knowledge. They have no speech; they use no words; no sound is heard from them. Yet their voice goes out into all the earth, their words to the ends of the world. In the heavens, God has pitched a tent for the sun.

It is like a bridegroom coming out of his chamber, like a champion rejoicing to run his course. It rises at one end of the heavens and makes its circuit to the other; nothing is deprived of its warmth."

"In whom the god of this world hath blinded the minds of them which believe not, lest the light of the glorious gospel of Christ, who is the image of God, should shine unto them". 2 Corinthians 4:4

In this passage, the sun is described as being like a bridegroom coming out of his chamber and like a champion rejoicing to run his course, attributing human characteristics to the sun. In the Torah, there are also instances where the sun and moon are personified or given human-like attributes, but the specific references may vary depending on interpretation and commentary. One example often cited is in Genesis 1:16-18, where God creates the sun and moon:

"God made the two great lights—the greater light to govern the day and the lesser light to govern the night. He also made the stars. God set them in the vault of the sky to give light on the earth, to govern the day and the night, and to separate light from darkness."

While this passage may not explicitly give human attributes to the sun and moon, some interpretations and commentaries may draw connections to human characteristics based on the role and functions assigned to these celestial bodies.

JOSEPH'S DREAM

The dream of the sun, the moon, and the eleven stars is often seen as a prophecy of Joseph's future rise to power and his family bowing down to him, which eventually came to pass. It is a story of forgiveness, redemption, and the fulfillment of divine plans despite the challenges and betrayals Joseph faced.

"The light of the body is the eye: if therefore thine eye be single, thy whole body shall be full of light. 23 But if thine eye be evil, thy whole body shall be full of darkness. If therefore the light that is in thee be darkness, how great is that darkness"! Matthew 6: 22-23

The story of Joseph and his dream of the sun, the moon, and the eleven stars is a significant episode in the Book of Genesis chapter 37, in the Bible.

Joseph was one of the twelve sons of Jacob (also known as Israel) and was favored by his father, which caused jealousy among his brothers. In the dream, Joseph sees the sun, the moon, and eleven stars bowing down to him. This dream is often interpreted symbolically, with the sun representing Joseph's father, the moon representing his mother, and the eleven stars representing his eleven brothers. The imagery of these celestial bodies bowing down to Joseph suggests a position of authority and power over his family.

Genesis 37:9

"Now he had still another dream, and related it to his brothers, and said, "Lo, I have had still another dream; and behold, the sun and the moon and eleven stars were bowing down to me."

Joseph's brothers, already envious of him due to their father's favoritism, interpreted the dream as a sign of Joseph's ambition to rule over them. This interpretation fueled their jealousy, leading them to conspire against Joseph. They eventually sold him into slavery and told their father that Joseph had been killed by a wild animal. Despite the hardships he faced, Joseph's life took a remarkable turn when he was eventually taken to Egypt and rose to a position of power through his interpretation of

dreams. His ability to interpret dreams caught the attention of the Pharaoh, who appointed him as a high-ranking official in Egypt.

"To open their eyes, and to turn them from darkness to light, and from the power of Satan unto God, that they may receive forgiveness of sins, and inheritance among them which are sanctified by faith that is in me", Acts 26:18

BEINGS- CELESTIAL, NOT HUMAN.

Years later, during a severe famine, Joseph's brothers came to Egypt seeking food.

They did not recognize Joseph, but he recognized them. Through a series of events, Joseph's dream became a reality.

While his father, who he dreamed was the sun, and his mother who he dreamed was the moon, were not real celestial beings. They were used symbolically in a prophetic manner. The fact that humans were depicted as celestial beings is evidence that celestial beings (the sun and the moon) can be depicted as human beings and written with having human attributes. By giving these celestial beings human attributes, most may interpret the writing to believe these beings are humans. While they are Beings, they are not human. In fact, this writer believes it is because of preconceived mindsets that most believe that the Two Witnesses are humans. As stated, several times before in this book, this writer believes the sun and the moon are the Two Witnesses, given human characteristics, for their assignments, at the appointed time of mourning. (sackcloth). Overall, the powers given to the two witnesses in Revelation symbolize their divine commission to bear witness to God's truth, to proclaim His judgment and mercy, and to demonstrate His authority over both the spiritual and natural realms during a time of tumultuous events leading up to the final judgment and the establishment of God's kingdom.

"The heavens declare the glory of God; and the firmament sheweth his handywork ".
Psalm 19:1

⭐ CHAPTER 8- ZECHARIAH'S ENCOUNTER

Zechariah 4 is a chapter in the Old Testament book of Zechariah that contains an unusual vision given to the prophet Zechariah. This is vison number 5 out of the 8 visions that was given to the prophet Zechariah. This vision was given at night and revolves around a golden lampstand, with seven lamps, a bowl, and two olive trees. Here is the dynamic scriptures in NIV and KJV version:

The Gold Lampstand and the Two Olive Trees NIV

Then the angel who talked with me returned and woke me up, like someone awakened from sleep. ² He asked me, "What do you see?"I answered, "I see a solid gold lampstand with a bowl at the top and seven lamps on it, with seven channels to the lamps. ³ Also there are two olive trees by it, one on the right of the bowl and the other on its left."⁴ I asked the angel who talked with me, **"What are these, my lord?"**⁵ He answered, "Do you not know what these are?""No, my lord," I replied. ⁶ So he said to me, "This is the word of the Lord to Zerubbabel: 'Not by might nor by power, but by my Spirit,' says the Lord Almighty."⁷ "What are you, mighty mountain? Before Zerubbabel you will become level ground. Then he will bring out the capstone to shouts of 'God bless it! God bless it!'"⁸ Then the word of the Lord came to me: ⁹ "The hands of Zerubbabel have laid the foundation of this temple; his hands will also complete it. Then you will know that the Lord Almighty has sent me to you.¹⁰ "Who dares despise the day of small things, since the seven eyes of the Lord that range throughout the earth will rejoice when they see the chosen capstone[a] in the hand of

Zerubbabel?"[11] Then I asked the angel, "What are these two olive trees on the right and the *left of the lampstand?*"[12] Again I asked him, "What are these two olive branches beside the two gold pipes that pour out golden oil?"[13] He replied, "Do you not know what these are?""No, my lord," I said.[14] So he said, **"These are the two who are anointed to**[b] **serve the Lord of all the earth."**

"The people that walked in darkness have seen a great light: they that dwell in the land of the shadow of death, upon them hath the light shined". Isaiah 9:2

The Gold Lampstand and the Two Olive Trees KJV

And the angel that talked with me came again, and waked me, as a man that is wakened out of his sleep.[2] And said unto me, What seest thou? And I said, I have looked, and behold a candlestick all of gold, with a bowl upon the top of it, and his seven lamps thereon, and seven pipes to the seven lamps, which are upon the top thereof:[3] And two olive trees by it, one upon the right side of the bowl, and the other upon the left side thereof.[4] So I answered and spake to the angel that talked with me, saying, **What are these, my lord**?[5] Then the angel that talked with me answered and said unto me, Knowest thou not what these be? And I said, No, my lord.[6] Then he answered and spake unto me, saying, This is the word of the LORD unto Zerubbabel, saying, Not by might, nor by power, but by my spirit, saith the LORD of hosts.[7] **Who art thou, O great mountain? before Zerubbabel thou shalt become a plain: and he shall bring forth the headstone thereof with shoutings, crying, Grace, grace unto it.**[8] Moreover the word of the LORD came unto me, saying,[9] The hands of Zerubbabel have laid the foundation of this house; his hands shall also finish it; and thou shalt know that the LORD of hosts hath sent me unto you.[10] For who hath despised the day of small things? for they shall rejoice, and shall see the plummet in the hand of Zerubbabel with those seven; they are the eyes of the LORD, which run to and fro through the whole earth.[11] Then answered I, and said unto him, What are these two olive trees upon the right side of the candlestick and upon the left side thereof?[12] And I answered again, and said unto him, What be these two olive branches which through the two golden pipes empty the golden oil out of themselves?[13] And he answered me and said, Knowest thou not what these be? And I said, No, my lord.[14] **Then said he, These are the two anointed ones, that stand by the LORD of the whole earth.**

The Book of Zechariah is dynamic in that it references a lot of history taken place prior to the events unfolding. To be able to understand each verse, one would have to be familiar with the history that took place prior to the angel visiting Zechariah. To be fair, even Zechariah was somewhat unsure as to what he was seeing in his encounter and asked the angel for clarification not once, but twice.

"We have also a more sure word of prophecy; whereunto ye do well that ye take heed, as unto a light that shineth in a dark place, until the day dawn, and the day star arise in your hearts:". 2 Peter 1:19

ZECHARIAH AND THE ANGEL

Zechariah 4:1-3: In these verses, Zechariah describes a vision of a golden lampstand with a bowl on top of it and seven lamps on it, with seven channels to the lamps. He also sees two olive trees, one on the right of the bowl and one on the left. To understand this let's envision what Zechariah is looking at., There is a golden lampstand with 7 channels that is going to the lamps, on top of it is a bowl, on the right is an olive tree, and another that is on the left.

Zechariah 4:4-6: After seeing the vision Zechariah was unsure of what he was seeing and ask the angel in verse 4, "What are these my lord"? Note the lowercase "l" in lord. Then the angel who was speaking with Zechariah somewhat ignores his question directly, and answers Zechariah's question with a question. The angel responds in verse 5 saying, "knowest not what these things be"? Zechariah answered that he did not know. The angel answers Zechariah's question and says "This is the word of the Lord to Zerubbabel".

WHO IS ZERUBBABEL

Zerubbabel was an intriguing and prominent figure in Jewish history. He was a leader of the Israelites and played the leading role in restoring the Second Temple in Jerusalem post the Babylonian exile era.

"He was a burning and a shining light: and ye were willing for a season to rejoice in his light". John 5:35

At a tumultuous time for the Jews, he was very significant in bringing faith driven leadership to the Israelites after their release from King Nebuchadnezzar, the Babylonian king.

He was given the arduous task of governing Judah by King Cyrus of Persia. It was his responsibility to lead, initiate, and oversee the reconstruction of the Temple.

This assignment was no easy task, and one that faced pushback, attacks, and intense prayer and faith in God. During this time

Zerubbabel was faced with extreme opposition from neighboring enemies. His level of determination, resilience, and devout faith in God during what seems to be impossible conditions, made him emerge a well-

respected leader that was victorious.

He was given a special promise by God, "as a signet ring", signifying divine purpose, favor, and honor. His accomplishment in successfully rebuilding the sacred Temple, at such a time, could only be God. Hence the Angel responding in Zechariah 4 :6 *"This is the word of the LORD unto Zerubbabel, saying, Not by might, nor by power, but by my spirit, saith the LORD of hosts".* Hallelujah! Reminding everyone that this accomplishment was due to the Spirit of God. Not man! Some things can ONLY be God! From the Blood line of David, and also the grandson of King Jehoiachin of Judah, Zerubbabel's positioning connects him to Old Testament law, and the Messianic promise of Jesus's return.

"I am come a light into the world, that whosoever believeth on me should not abide in darkness". John 12:46

WHAT ARE THESE TWO?

Still confused about the vision before him, Zechariah asks the angel again about the two olive trees on either side of the lampstand. The angel answers directly this time. Which the angel finally responds, *"These are the two who are anointed to serve the Lord of all the earth"* King James version says, *"Then said he, These are the two anointed ones, that stand by the LORD of the whole earth".* This writer observed in both edition, the lampstand and the olive tree was referred to as "These Two", this is consistent in Revelation as well.

Then I asked the angel, "What are these two olive trees on the right and the left of the lampstand?"¹² Again I asked him, "What are these two olive branches beside the two gold pipes that pour out golden oil?"¹³ He replied, "Do you not know what these are?" "No, my lord," I said.¹⁴ So he said, "These are the two who are anointed to[b] serve the Lord of all the earth."

"What" are these two, "What" be these two, is much different from, WHO are these two. Let's pay attention to verse 14 as well.

The angel said to Zechariah that these are the two anointed ones that "stand by the lord of the whole earth". Notice he did not say that they would come, or that they would stand. Rather that they, "stand by the Lord of the whole Earth". It is very clear that the two anointed ones are already presently standing by the Lord of the whole Earth. They are already there, just not given the power to minister as yet. The vision of the lampstand and the olive trees are consistent symbols in the Old and New Testament of the apocalyptic timing, divine empowerment and guidance provided by God to accomplish His purposes through Jesus.

"The statutes of the Lord are right, rejoicing the heart: the commandment of the Lord is pure, enlightening the eyes". Psalm 19:8

The significance of the one lampstand, versus the two, that was revealed by John in Revelation is not clear. Is it because the Jews were blinded (night) by God? Were the two branches pouring the oil into the lamp due to the historical significance of the Menorah (which is Hebrew for lamp), within the Tabernacle? The ancient Menorah had 7 branches, for each day of creation.

Is the oil being poured into the bowl significant of the ancient Temple, where the oil in the lamp was to continue to burn and not run out?

Is the bowl atop the Lampstand the prayer bowl that Jews used in the past to ward off evil? What does it mean atop of the one lamp stand? So many questions. Does the one lampstand represent the Torah or Old Testament? Does the 2 Lampstand in Revelation represent both the Old and the New Testament? It is unclear. What is clear, is that it will make sense, at that time. What is also very clear is, the world needs the True Light, both day and night, in order to see.

"Rejoice not against me, O mine enemy: when I fall, I shall arise; when I sit in darkness, the Lord shall be a light unto me". Micah 7:8

⭐ CHAPTER 9- CONTEXT- MATTER- BREAK - BUILD- SPIRIT

In the Bible, the use of symbolism versus literal translation is an important aspect of understanding the various genres, writing styles, and intended messages found within its pages. The Bible contains a diverse range of literature, including historical narratives, poetry, prophecy, parables, letters, and apocalyptic visions, each requiring different approaches to interpretation. Let's break it down by examining the symbolic, literal, metaphorical, and even the historical context in translation. These changes matter in how many understand individually, or how it is taught collectively.

SYMBOLISM, LITERALISM AND METAPHORS- CONTEXT MATTERS

The Bible consists of many different levels of symbolism. Readers have to use context clues, history and most definitely the leadership of the

Holy Spirit when reading. Oftentimes one passage can have different meaning, at different times, for different individuals.

This can be effective and acceptable to an individual, however, not to be used out of context. This is a slippery slope I am aware. His word is alive, and the Spirit of God brings light and revelation. This is why it is very important to pray when reading. In this same Bible, is symbolism, literalism, and metaphorical writing that takes light to understand.

"The LORD lift up his countenance upon thee, and give thee peace.". Numbers 6:26

One example of symbolic writing is the use of parables. A parable is a simple story used to tell a point or to illustrate a lesson. Jesus frequently used parables to teach spiritual truths using everyday scenarios that his audience could relate to. For instance, the Parable of the Good Samaritan in Luke 10:25-37. Jesus used symbolic characters to convey the message of loving one's neighbor.

Another example of symbolism is prophetic writing. Prophetic books like Daniel and Revelation often employ vivid imagery and symbolism to convey messages about future events, spiritual truths, and the ultimate triumph of God over evil forces.

The Song of Solomon is an allegorical love poem that symbolizes the relationship between God and His people or Christ and the Church. Allegories are another form of symbolic writing, and intense might I add. Song of Solomon chapter 4 is as passionate as they come. Let's look at verse 16. Intense and pure beauty.

"Awake, O north wind; and come, thou south; blow upon my garden, that the spices thereof may flow out. Let my beloved come into his garden, and eat his pleasant fruits".

Another example of symbolic writing in the scripture Throughout the Bible, metaphors and similes', are used to describe God, Jesus, and spiritual concepts. For example, Jesus referred to himself as the "vine" and his followers as the "branches" in John 15:1-8. Revelation use of simile in the Bible such as where it stated,

"13 And in the midst of the seven candlesticks one like unto the Son of man, clothed with a garment down to the foot, and girt about the paps with a golden girdle. 14 His head and his hairs were white like wool, as white as snow; and his eyes were as a flame of fire; 15 And his feet like unto fine brass, as if they burned in a furnace; and his voice as the sound of many waters. 16 And he had in his right hand seven stars: and out of his mouth went a sharp twoedged sword: and his countenance was as the sun shineth in his strength".

"But the path of the just is as the shining light, that shineth more and more unto the perfect day". Proverbs 4:18

Sometimes it's difficult to differentiate what is symbolic from actual literal writings in Biblical text. Proving literal truths requires investigation of facts. Some will argue that all of the Bible is fantasy, those without faith. Whereas you have others like this writer who maintains that all of the Bible is truth. However, due to the different writing styles in the Bible, science, historical narratives, and of course faith, one can get a better understanding of what God is saying through His various writers.

Many parts of the Bible present straightforward historical accounts of events, such as the creation story in Genesis, the Exodus from Egypt, and the life of Jesus as recorded in the Gospels. There are other factors that needs to be taken into consideration when understanding Literalism in the Bible, such as the Ten Commandments.

The Ten Commandments and other moral teachings in the Bible are meant to be understood and followed as direct commands from God without symbolic interpretation.

Genealogy is another factor when considering literal meaning when reading the scriptures. Dates, location, times and seasons found in the Bible, is very specific and not to be taken metaphorically or symbolically. Lineage list the timing and order of birth and death of individuals in a literal and factual manner, establishing family connections and historical continuity.

Understanding the balance between symbolism and literal translation is crucial for interpreting the Bible accurately.

"This then is the message which we have heard of him, and declare unto you, that God is light, and in him is no darkness at all". 1 John 1:5

It requires careful consideration of the context, awareness of cultural background, literary style, and authorial (God) intent of each passage, at the time written.

Some passages are rich in symbolism and metaphor, inviting readers to explore deeper meanings and spiritual truths, while others are intended to be taken at face value as historical accounts, moral teachings, or direct commands. By approaching the Bible with a discerning eye for symbolism and literalism, readers can engage with its diverse genres and messages more effectively, gaining a deeper understanding of its timeless truths and teachings.

SYMBOLISM AND LITERALISM IN REVELATION

The Book of Revelation, the final book of the New Testament, is a highly symbolic and enigmatic text that has fascinated and perplexed readers, scholars, and theologians for centuries. Its apocalyptic imagery, vivid visions, and complex symbolism have led to a wide range of interpretations regarding whether that specific book, chapter or even the verse, should be read as primarily symbolic or as a literal description of future events. Differentiating when to switch over is helpful. Pray. Allow the Holy Spirit to guide you.

Symbolism in the Book of Revelation is on every single page, within almost ever single verse. The reader has to pray intently and prepare to read. Each page employs a rich tapestry of symbols, numbers, and imagery to convey its message.

"Thy sun shall no more go down; neither shall thy moon withdraw itself: for the Lord shall be thine everlasting light, and the days of thy mourning shall be ended". Isaiah 60:20

Symbolism is a prominent feature of apocalyptic literature, which often uses figurative language to communicate spiritual truths, cosmic conflicts, and eschatological themes.

Focusing on the key symbols such as the seven seals, seven trumpets, seven bowls, the four horsemen of the apocalypse, the beast, the dragon, the woman clothed with the sun, and many others, is of importance as each symbol has deep meaning and

revelation in and of itself. Historically these symbols are open to a variety of translation and interpretations and are believed to represent deeper spiritual realities rather than literal descriptions from most theologians and Bible scholars.

Literal Interpretation of the Book of Revelation by some scholars and theologians advocate for a more direct interpretation of certain elements, especially concerning prophecies about the end times and the Second Coming of Christ. That is because interpretations vary based on knowledge and light. Sometimes the same scripture can have different interpretation to the same reader, based on revelation. Proponents of literal interpretation often focus on identifying connections between the symbols in Revelation and real-world events and will construct a timeline of future events based on the text. There is no doubt that the book of Revelation has inspired a wide range of interpretations across Christian traditions and scholarly circles. Different theological perspectives, hermeneutical approaches, and historical contexts have shaped how readers and scholars understand the book.

" **For every one that doeth evil hateth the light, neither cometh to the light, lest his deeds should be reproved". John 3:20**

As mentioned earlier in this chapter, some interpretations may differ. Some may even say this writer's interpretation is biased, based on faith. Guilty. This writer in fact does blend symbolism with literal elements, recognizing the dual nature of apocalyptic features plus the complexity of the text. Other writers may emphasize one approach over the other, leading to diverse and sometimes conflicting interpretations of the book. However, again, allowing the Holy Spirit to lead and guide works best. Not everything is logical. In fact, sometimes, it makes absolutely no sense at all. Think about it, we don't plan to be here after the rapture anyway. Do you?

BREAK IT DOWN

HISTORICAL STUDY AND REVELATION

Time is one of those things that can make absolutely no sense. It's a good thing we understand that things of the spirit oftentimes, seems illogical. It's also a good thing that we know what Brother Peter wrote about time. 2 Peter 3:8, "But beloved, be not ignorant of this one thing, that one day is with the Lord as a thousand years, and a thousand years as one day". Hallelujah! So even though historical perspectives, various individuals, and groups have interpreted the Book of Revelation in different ways, oftentimes reflecting the cultural, political, and religious contexts of their time, interpretation can be different. It may even also appear at times, biased.

[4] "**And God saw the light, that it was good: and God divided the light from the darkness**". **Genesis 1: 4**

Interpretations have ranged from seeing Revelation as a coded critique of the Roman Empire to viewing it as a roadmap for future end-time events. The diversity of interpretations of Revelation highlights its enduring relevance and the ongoing quest to unravel its mysteries and uncover its profound messages, again, led by the Holy Spirit. The Book of Revelation is a multifaceted and challenging text that invites readers to engage with its symbolism, imagery, and themes in diverse ways. Whether approached primarily as symbolic or literal, the book continues to provoke contemplation, debate, and fascination as one of the most enigmatic and powerful works of apocalyptic literature in the Christian tradition.

In the book of Revelation, Chapter 11, verses 3-13, the Two Witnesses are described as granted prophetic authority by God during the end times. As stated previously, some believe this to be two end time prophets that were previously here before, and written about in the Old Testament. Many scholars and theologians hold this stance. This writer disagrees and challenges that theory of the Two Witnesses being O.T prophets or human beings for that matter, but support the idea of celestial beings that are already here. They, the sun and the moon will testify, based on what will be happening. They in and of themselves will BE a testament of His power before the final judgment.

"Giving thanks to the Father, who has qualified you to share in the inheritance of the saints in light" Colossians 1:12 ESV

BREAK DOWN TO BUILD UP

The poetic flow of the writing, the specific choice of wording, the change that took place from literal to metaphoric to figurative, all had to be taken into consideration and put into context. Well, because context matters.

While God wrote the book, through John, it is people that have played it out, will play it out, and are currently playing it out, due to free will. All in all, God's Word is true. All of it! As we move forward let's look closer at the natural behavior, characteristics, purpose and significance of the two witnesses in Revelation: Here are the key points outlining how the Two Witnesses represent prophetic authority in the context of Revelation:

1. Prophetic Mission and Authority: The two witnesses are described as having authority to prophesy for 1,260 days, clothed in sackcloth,

which is understood symbolically as a period of intense tribulation or persecution.

They are described as two olive trees and two lampstands standing before the Lord of the earth. This imagery is reminiscent of the prophets Zechariah with the angel from the Old Testament. Their role is to bear witness to God's truth and to proclaim His judgments upon the earth. Notice the language used, "give power", meaning they are there, just not given the power to begin their prophetic ministry as yet.

"**3 And they that be wise shall shine as the brightness of the firmament; and they that turn many to righteousness as the stars for ever and ever" Daniel 12:3**

Revelation 11: 3-4 "And I will give power unto my two witnesses, and they shall prophesy a thousand two hundred and threescore days, clothed in sackcloth. 4 These are the two olive trees, and the two candlesticks standing before the God of the earth".

2. <u>Symbolic Identity:</u> The specific identities of the two witnesses are subject to much speculation and interpretation. Some interpretations suggest that they could represent Old Testament figures, who performed miracles and confronted evil in the biblical narratives. Others view them as symbolic representations of the Church or the Word of God.

This writer challenges that view. The symbolism of the 2 Olive Tree represents the sun, which is used to grow the Olive Trees by way of photosynthesis.

Photosynthesis is the transfer of energy from the sun's light to the plants and can only occur in the presence of the sun. Which is why plants need the sun, hence the Olive Tree, in order to produce fruit, it must have sunlight. The 2 Candlestick or Lampstand represents the moon, which is used for illumination during the night.

Candlestick and Lampstand is the necessity of seeing your way in the dark, at night. One would not use or need a lampstand or candlestick where there is sunlight. Genesis reminds us, as mentioned before, that the sun would "rule" or "govern" the day, and the moon would "rule" or "govern" the night. The Holy Scripture was very clear in describing the identity of the Two Witnesses, by way of their functions, and where they are located. They are located, "standing before God of the earth".

[6] **And he said, It is a light thing that thou shouldest be my servant to raise up the tribes of Jacob, and to restore the preserved of Israel: I will also give thee for a light to the Gentiles, that thou mayest be my salvation unto the end of the earth. Isaiah 49:6.**

3. <u>Miraculous Powers</u>: The two witnesses are granted supernatural abilities to perform miracles, during their prophetic ministry. Miracles such as calling down fire from heaven and causing various plagues. These miraculous signs serve to authenticate their message and to demonstrate the power and authority of God working through them. They have the ability to strike the earth with plagues as often as they want and to consume their enemies with fire from their mouths. These miraculous acts demonstrate their authority and authenticity as is sovereign.

Weather conditions are contingent upon the sun and the moon as well. Scientists believe that the earth's alignment with the sun and the moon and the gravitational pull, creates a tidal force, and results in high or low tide, and that can create the way in which bodies of water can respond. Based on the behavior of the sun and the moon, famine, plagues, and disaster can happen on earth, and in the seas.

Revelation 11:5-6 "If anyone wants to harm them, fire comes out of their mouths and devours their enemies. In this way, anyone wanting to harm them is sure to be slain. 6They have the power to close up the sky so that no rain can fall during the time of their prophesying".

"**²⁷ The spirit of man is the candle of the LORD, searching all the inward parts of the belly**" **Proverbs 20:27**

4. <u>Opposition, Persecution, and Martyrdom:</u> The two witnesses face fierce opposition from the forces of evil, symbolized by the beast that rises from the bottomless pit.

This beast overcomes and kills them, and their bodies lie in the street of the great city . of Jerusalem for three and a half days as a sign of contempt and victory over them. As to the how and the why this occurs requires prophetic lens. This writer believes the beast to be a system, just as the "mark of the beast" is public acceptance, and allegiance to the anti-Christ system.

BUILD UP-SPIRIT

4. Symbolic Representation: The Two Witnesses are often interpreted symbolically in various ways. Some see them as representing the Old Testament and the New Testament, while others view them as symbolic of the Church or specific historical figures. Regardless of the interpretation, they are seen as figures of prophetic authority and testimony in the midst of great turmoil and tribulation.

They appear in the Old and New Testament as the 2 Olive Tree and 2 Candlestick (One Candlestick in Zechariah) in Revelation.

SPIRIT

5. <u>Resurrection and Ascension</u>: (For this section, grab your prophetic lens again, it requires imagination and faith). After lying dead for three and a half days, the two witnesses are resurrected and taken up to heaven in a cloud, signaling their victory over death and their vindication by God. This event causes great fear and awe among those who witness it, leading some to repent and turn to God.

"**14 Wherefore he saith, Awake thou that sleepest, and arise from the dead, and Christ shall give thee light**". Ephesians 5:14

Hopefully you still have on your prophetic lens, because it is required to understand this section. The breath of life from God is a quickening or spiritual energy.

This writer struggled with understanding this section until the Lord reminded me of what I witnessed at the bedside of a family member that was passing. The room was filled with people, and everyone was crying and emotional. I was standing at her bedside on the left, by her head. I watched as my aunt breathed out her last breath.

Moments later I witnessed a round light leaving my aunt's body. There was an actual orb that was leaving my aunt's body and ascending upwards. At the time, I didn't know there was a name for it, until I later did research and found out. I noticed it and simply couldn't take my eyes off of what I was seeing. I shared this with those who were in the room.

No one else had seen it. The orb was translucent and appeared as small as a pearl. It was iridescent in color of pearl, pink, purple, onyx, cream and extremely beautiful. It was spinning and looked almost like a bubble that could be popped.

I watched it leave from what appeared on the top or back of her head and kept going up, up into the air, until it disappeared. The Lord allowing me to see that was a gift and gave me complete peace, since her and I were very close. It was that memory that the Lord showed me, after praying and asking Him to help me to understand verse 11.

"The people that walked in darkness have seen a great light: they that dwell in the land of the shadow of death, upon them hath the light shined". Isaiah 9:2

It is that same energy force, spirit, orb, whatever you want to call it, that force, the "breath of life" from God spoken about in Genesis 2:7 that will enter into these heavenly bodies that littered the earth that would create a phenomenon so unusual that it would absolutely frighten, dumbfound and change the stubborn mindset of some of those who did not believe the God of the Bible.

As in the days of Genesis, where God spoke things into creation and into being, He will speak to His creation again. This time saying, "Come up hither", and His creation will obey the voice of God. People will see, and marvel at what is happening, and change.

> *Revelation 11 verse 11-13 "11 And after three days and an half the spirit of life from God entered into them, and they stood upon their feet; and great fear fell upon them which saw them. 12 And they heard a great voice from heaven saying unto them, Come up hither. And they ascended up to heaven in a cloud; and their enemies beheld them. 13 And the same hour was there a great earthquake, and the tenth part of the city fell, and in the earthquake were slain of men seven thousand: and the remnant were affrighted, and gave glory to the God of heaven.*

Breath of Life is found in Genesis 2:7 "*Then the LORD God formed a man[c] from the dust of the ground and breathed into his nostrils the breath of life, and the man became a living being.*

6. <u>Symbolism, Metaphorical, and Literalism:</u> The story of the two witnesses is rich in apocalyptic imagery, reflecting themes of faithful witness, persecution, martyrdom, resurrection, and divine judgment.

"While ye have light, believe in the light, that ye may be the children of light. These things spake Jesus, and departed, and did hide himself from them". John 12:36

The focus of this writing is to introduce readers to the idea that while there is much symbolism, and metaphor in the Bible and specifically in the Book of Revelation, the Two Witnesses, their function, character, and their behavior is not symbolic, but however definitely literal. However, it requires faith in God, and knowing and believing that not everything in this world is visible by seeing, but by sight. **John 4:24 KJV:** *God is a Spirit: and they that worship him must worship him in spirit and in truth.*

7. <u>Interpretation</u>: Interpretations of this passage vary widely among

theologians and scholars, with some emphasizing the historical context of the early Christian Church and others focusing on eschatological events leading up to the end times. The interpretation of the two witnesses in Revelation as the sun and the moon is not a common or widely

accepted interpretation within mainstream Christian theology. While writing to date, I have never heard anyone else suggest, or mention this. The eclipse on April 8, 2024, and knowing what the Lord told me, and receiving what I believe was a release to write, assured me it was time to write this down. So here it is, in this book. Based on what was revealed by the Holy Spirit, to this writer. It's important to remember that God called the Sun and the Moon "two great lights," and that meanwhile the text highlights their importance in the divine plan of creation, symbolizing God's power, wisdom, and creative design. These celestial bodies serve as reminders of God's presence, authority, and provision in the world, guiding and sustaining life on Earth through their light and influence.

"[9] **If I take the wings of the morning, and dwell in the uttermost parts of the sea;** [10] **Even there shall thy hand lead me, and thy right hand shall hold me.** [11] **If I say, Surely the darkness shall cover me; even the night shall be light about me". Psalm 139:9-11**

Overall, the two witnesses in Revelation serves as powerful testament of God's faithfulness, the call to prophetic witness in the face of opposition, and the ultimate victory of God's kingdom over the forces of evil.

The language used in this passage conveys the majesty, purpose, and beauty of the Sun and the Moon as integral parts of God's creation, showcasing their roles as sources of light, markers of time, and symbols of divine order and providence. However, let us never forget the One True Everlasting Light, the Creator of the sun and the moon. All glory and honor to God.

"That was the true Light, which lighteth every man that cometh into the world".John 1:9

★ Chapter 10 God The Everlasting Light- DNA

The concept of God as light is a recurring theme in the Bible, the Torah, and the Tanakh. Every page in this book is headed with a scripture that reminds us of the True Light. While the sun and the moon are luminaries and are believed to be the true witnesses, as this writer continue to remind readers. This does not take away from the Creator of the Two Witnesses, whomever one may believe the Two Witnesses to be. It is extremely important to remember, reverence, honor, glorify and give complete appreciation to Jesus Christ, son of the One True Almighty God, the Everlasting Light. Glory to God!

The concept of "everlasting light" as mentioned in Isaiah can be understood through the teachings of both the Torah (the foundational text of Judaism) and the Bible (which includes the Old Testament shared by Judaism and Christianity). This theme of everlasting light conveys the idea of God's enduring presence, glory, and illumination that will shine eternally in the lives of believers. Drawing both from the Torah and using Biblical reference we will see the connection and the uniformed message that God is light.

In the Torah, light is often associated with God's presence and guidance. For example, in Exodus 13:21, during the Israelites' journey through the wilderness, the Lord guided them with a pillar of cloud by day and a pillar of fire by night. This imagery of light symbolized God's constant presence and direction.

The same came for a witness, to bear witness of the Light, that all men through him might believe". John 1:7

The Torah emphasizes the importance of following God's commandments to walk in the light of His truth and wisdom.

Psalm 119:105 states, "Your word is a lamp to my feet and a light to my path," highlighting the Torah's role in being used by God to illuminate the way for believers.

Psalm 119:105 is a well-known verse that holds deep significance in the context of faith and guidance. Let's break down this scripture and explore its meaning from both a theological and scholarly perspective, including insights from the Torah:

Psalm 119:105 (New International Version)

A. Your word is a lamp for my feet:

This part of the verse emphasizes the illuminating and guiding power of God's Word. It's clearly telling us that God's teachings, instructions, and commandments provide clarity and direction for one's immediate steps or decisions.

The imagery of a lamp for one's feet evokes the idea of a light source that illuminates the path directly ahead, preventing stumbling or going astray.

B. A light on my path:

This phrase extends the metaphor of guidance further, allowing the reader to understand that God's Word serves as a broader source of light that illuminates the entire path of life. It signifies divine wisdom, truth, and insight that guide believers in their journey through life. The light on the path symbolizes God's presence, leading believers along the right course and revealing the way forward amidst darkness or uncertainty.

"The sun shall be no more thy light by day; neither for brightness shall the moon give light unto thee: but the Lord shall be unto thee an everlasting light, and thy God thy glory". Isaiah 60:19

The verse underscores the importance of Scripture and divine revelation as a source of guidance and illumination in the life of a believer. It highlights the transformative power of God's Word to provide direction, wisdom, and comfort in times of need.

The metaphorical language used in the verse reflects the intimate relationship between the believer and God, portraying God as a light that dispels darkness and shows the way to righteousness and truth.

TORAH LIGHT AND BIBLICAL LIGHT

Scholars and theologians often interpret Psalm 119:105 in the context of the Torah, Hebrew Bible, and Jewish teachings, emphasizing the centrality of God's Word in Jewish faith and practice.

The verse is seen as a reflection of the Jewish tradition's reverence for the Torah as a source of divine instruction, moral guidance, and spiritual illumination. Scholars may explore the historical and cultural significance of light imagery in Jewish thought, drawing connections to the menorah in the Temple, the concept of the Shekhinah (divine presence), and the role of Torah study in Jewish life.

Psalm 119:105 conveys a profound message about the transformative power of God's Word as a guiding light in the life of believers. It serves as a reminder of the importance of seeking divine wisdom and direction through Scripture, illuminating the path of righteousness and faithfulness.

"Give glory to the Lord your God, before he cause darkness, and before your feet stumble upon the dark mountains, and, while ye look for light, he turn it into the shadow of death, and make it gross darkness". Jeremiah 13:16

In the Bible, particularly in the Book of Isaiah, the theme of everlasting light is a promise of God's eternal presence and glory. Isaiah 60:19-20 prophesies a future time when God Himself will be the everlasting light of His people, replacing the need for the sun and the moon.

"The sun will no more be your light by day, nor will the brightness of the moon shine on you, for the LORD will be your everlasting light, and your God will be your glory. [20] Your sun will never set again, and your moon will wane no more; the LORD will be your everlasting light, and your days of sorrow will end".

This concept is further developed in the New Testament, where Jesus is often referred to as the light of the world. In John 8:12, Jesus declares, "I am the light of the world. Whoever follows me will never walk in darkness but will have the light of life." Genesis 1:3: In the creation account, God said, "Let there be light," and there was light. This demonstrates God's power and authority over light and darkness, symbolizing His role as the source of all light and illumination. The Bible teaches that through faith in Jesus Christ, believers receive the light of salvation and eternal life. 2 Corinthians 4:6 says, "For God, who said, 'Let light shine out of darkness,' made his light shine in our hearts to give us the light of the knowledge of God's glory displayed in the face of Christ."

By combining insights from the Torah and the Bible, we see that the concept of everlasting light represents God's unchanging presence, guidance, and salvation for His people. It signifies His eternal nature, wisdom, and glory that illuminates the path of

believers and brings hope for a future filled with His light and love. This everlasting light points to the ultimate fulfillment of God's promises and the restoration of all things in His eternal kingdom.

"The spirit of man is the candle of the Lord, searching all the inward parts of the belly". Proverbs 20:27

Psalm 27:1 "The Lord is my light and my salvation—whom shall I fear? The Lord is the stronghold of my life—of whom shall I be afraid?" This verse highlights God as a source of light and salvation, dispelling fear and darkness. Psalm 36:9 "For with you is the fountain of life; in your light we see light." This verse emphasizes God's role as the source of life and light, enabling us to see truth and walk in His ways. Isaiah 60:19: "The sun will no more be your light by day, nor will the brightness of the moon shine on you, for the Lord will be your everlasting light, and your God will be your glory." This verse from the Book of Isaiah portrays God as an everlasting light that surpasses the natural lights of the sun and moon. John 8:12: Jesus refers to Himself as the light of the world: "I am the light of the world. Whoever follows me will never walk in darkness, but will have the light of life." This statement emphasizes Jesus as the embodiment of God's light and truth.

D.N.A. MADE IN HIS IMAGE-LIGHT

God as light conveys various meanings, including illumination, guidance, truth, purity, and salvation. It symbolizes God's presence, glory, and transformative power in the lives of believers. We are reminded in John 4:24 (NIV) that "God is a spirit. Those who worship him must worship in spirit and truth". We are also reminded in Genesis 1:27 that "So God created mankind in his own image, in the image of God he created them; male and female he created them". Since man is created in the image of God, we are spiritual beings, as well as earthly vessels. Mankind is flesh, wrapped in spirit, and once saved, the spirit of God. (Remember the story of my aunt and the orb). Glory to God!

"For God, who commanded the light to shine out of darkness, hath shined in our hearts, to give the light of the knowledge of the glory of God in the face of Jesus Christ". 2 Corinthians 4:6

Romans 8:22-27 NIV

[22] We know that the whole creation has been groaning as in the pains of childbirth right up to the present time. [23] Not only so, but we ourselves, who have the firstfruits of the Spirit, groan inwardly as we wait eagerly for our adoption to sonship, the redemption of our bodies. [24] For in this hope we were saved. But hope that is seen is no hope at all. Who hopes for what they already have? [25] But if we hope for what we do not yet have, we wait for it patiently.

[26] In the same way, the Spirit helps us in our weakness. We do not know what we ought to pray for, but the Spirit himself intercedes for us through wordless groans. [27] And he who searches our hearts knows the mind of the Spirit, because the Spirit intercedes for God's people in accordance with the will of God.

These references demonstrate the rich biblical imagery of God as light, highlighting His role as the ultimate source of illumination, goodness, and salvation for those who seek Him. How are His creation affected by lack of light?

The scripture tells us over and over again, that lack of light is darkness. However, the answer is found in Christ.John 8:12. Jesus tell us clearly,

"*12 When Jesus spoke again to the people, he said, "I am the light of the world. Whoever follows me will never walk in darkness, but will have the light of life".*

Hallelujah!

PHYSICAL EFFECTS OF THE Other lights

"*9 That was the true Light, which lighteth every man that cometh into the world*". John 1:9. Jesus was the true light, He made that very clear. We will now look into the other lights.

"For, behold, the darkness shall cover the earth, and gross darkness the people: but the LORD shall arise upon thee, and his glory shall be seen upon thee". Isaiah 60:2

Not the "True", "Everlasting", light, but, the other lights. The "two great lights", created on day four. God is a God of purpose. He does not do anything irrelevant. Why are the other lights physically necessary for mankind? What is the importance of the two?

While the Sun and the Moon are not directly related to biology in the same way they are in astronomy and nature, their influence on Earth's ecosystems and organisms cannot be overlooked.

Here are some ways in which the Sun and the Moon play important biological roles:

Sunlight is essential for photosynthesis, the process by which plants and some other organisms convert light energy into chemical energy. This process is the foundation of the food chain, as plants produce oxygen and organic compounds that sustain all life on Earth. Sunlight influences plant growth, flowering, and fruiting cycles. The intensity and duration of sunlight regulate the rate of photosynthesis and, consequently, the productivity of ecosystems, and the physical systems of humans.

Circadian Rhythms and Biological Clocks are affected by the Sun and the Moon. Think for a minute how complex and highly strategic our Creator. There is an interconnection with the sun, the moon, they play a role in regulating circadian rhythms, which are internal clocks that control biological processes such as sleep-wake cycles, hormone production, and metabolism in organisms.

Sunlight helps synchronize circadian rhythms by signaling to organisms when it is time to be awake and active.

>[5] **And God called the light Day, and the darkness he called Night. And the evening and the morning were the first day". Genesis 1:5**

Sunlight is essential for the production of vitamin D in human skin, which directly and indirectly affects mood. This vitamin plays a crucial role in calcium absorption, bone health, and immune function, highlighting the biological importance of sunlight exposure for human health, too much sunlight can become detrimental. Moonlight as well, especially during the full moon, can also influence the behavior of some nocturnal animals. Hence the saying of people acting "weird" in a full moon. God is simply amazing.

It is amazing just how much these two affect the biology of humans, and the behavior of what happens on Earth. There are times, when science and religion agree. In fact, science is catching up, to what has already been prophesied in the Word of God.

The gravitational pull of the Moon influences ocean tides, which create dynamic coastal habitats that support diverse marine life.

Tidal movements help distribute nutrients, oxygen, and plankton, which are essential for marine ecosystems.

Some marine organisms, such as certain species of fish and crustaceans, have evolved to synchronize their reproductive cycles with lunar phases, using moonlight as a cue for spawning activities. This phenomenon is important to remember, because during their prophetic administration, Revelation speaks to the changes in the seas, and in the weather. The changing angle and intensity of sunlight with the seasons, trigger biological responses in many organisms, such as hibernation, migration, and breeding behaviors. Some animals rely on the position of the Sun and stars for navigation during long-distance migrations, while others use the Moon's phases to time their movements or reproductive activities.

12 even the darkness will not be dark to you; the night will shine like the day, for darkness is as light to you". Isaiah 139:12

While the Sun and the Moon may not be biological entities themselves, their influence on Earth's ecosystems, organisms, and biological processes is profound and multifaceted.

These celestial bodies shape the rhythms of life on our planet and will play crucial roles during this time. In fact, they will be the lead Actors.

"for the fruit of light is found in all that is good and right and true". Ephesians 5:9 ESV

⭐ CHAPTER 11- QUEUE, BETTER YET, CUE THE ANOINTED NIGHT LIGHT

"When I consider Your heavens, the work of Your fingers, The moon and the stars, which You have ordained" Psalm 8:3

The symbolism of the two olive trees and the two candlesticks is found in the Book of Revelation 11:4. Candlesticks or lampstands are often used in the Bible as symbols of light, truth, and the presence of God. As previously discussed, this image is symbolic for the Two Witnesses, who this writer has expressly shared multiple times in this book to be the sun and the moon.

However, Revelation 11:4 is not the only place in scripture where the Candlestick or Lampstand, and the Olive Tree /(s) is mentioned prior to being mentioned in Revelation 11. The Candlestick, or Lampstand was also mentioned in Zecharia 4 (discussed in Chapter 8 -" Zechariah's Encounter"), Revelation 1, and Revelation 4. Let's look closer at how the Candlestick and Lampstand shows up, in Revelation 1 and in Revelation 4. Does their appearance signify an assignment, role, function, or meaning? Nothing is coincidence, or by chance.

Revelation 1: 10-20

"[10] On the Lord's Day I was in the Spirit, and I heard behind me a loud voice like a trumpet, [11] which said: "Write on a scroll what you see and send it to the seven churches: to Ephesus, Smyrna, Pergamum, Thyatira, Sardis, Philadelphia and Laodicea."[12] I turned around to see the voice that was speaking to me.

"[36] If thy whole body therefore be full of light, having no part dark, the whole shall be full of light, as when the bright shining of a candle doth give thee light". Luke 11:36

And when I turned I saw seven golden lampstands, ¹³ and among the lampstands was someone like a son of man,[d] dressed in a robe reaching down to his feet and with a golden sash around his chest.

¹⁴ The hair on his head was white like wool, as white as snow, and his eyes were like blazing fire. ¹⁵ His feet were like bronze glowing in a furnace, and his voice was like the sound of rushing waters. ¹⁶ In his right hand he held seven stars, and coming out of his mouth was a sharp, double-edged sword. His face was like the sun shining in all its brilliance. ¹⁷ When I saw him, I fell at his feet as though dead. Then he placed his right hand on me and said: "Do not be afraid. I am the First and the Last. ¹⁸ I am the Living One; I was dead, and now look, I am alive for ever and ever! And I hold the keys of death and Hades.

¹⁹ "Write, therefore, what you have seen, what is now and what will take place later. ²⁰ The mystery of the seven stars that you saw in my right hand and of the seven golden lampstands is this: The seven stars are the angels[e] of the seven churches, and the seven lampstands are the seven churches.

COMMON THEME

The vision of the seven golden lampstands is described in Revelation 1:10-20, where Jesus is depicted walking among the lampstands. It is important to note in this particular passage, the lampstand is representative of the seven churches in Asia.

"The seven stars are the angels of the seven churches, and the seven lampstands are the seven churches".

Right here in Revelation 1 the, "mystery of the seven stars that you saw in my right hand, and of the seven golden lampstands" is explained. The scripture tells us plainly that the seven stars are the angels or messengers of those seven churches.

Who hath delivered us from the power of darkness, and hath translated us into the kingdom of his dear Son: Colossians 1:13

Those seven churches, who are represented here as the Lampstand/Candlestick have been identified in Revelation 1 as the "seven churches in the province of Asia". Those churches listed in Revelation 1:11 are Ephesus, Smyrna, Pergamum, Thyatira, Sardis, Philadelphia, and Laodicea.

The candlesticks in Revelation serves as a symbol of light, truth, and the presence of God among His people.

Jesus's presence among the lampstands in Revelation 1: 12 signifies His intimate involvement with and care for the churches, as well as His role as the Savior. Jesus walking alongside the lampstand, is clear that He is with the church, and the church is anointed for ministry.

The Church collectively, as the body of Christ, and church individually, as the living temple, epistle, the ecclesia, the called out ones.

The lampstand is later mentioned again in Revelation 4:5, "in front of the throne". The positioning and location of the seven lamps in front of The Anointed One, is indicative that this is a place of pure Sovereignty, and divine worship. There seated at the throne is God. The 24 elders seated before the throne continually bow to Him, recognizing and reverencing that this is a sacred place, and He is the Anointed Sacred One who holds power, majesty, dominion and is to be exalted in total and continuous worship Hallelujah!

"To give light to them that sit in darkness and in the shadow of death, to guide our feet into the way of peace". Luke 1:79

As discussed, the imagery of the seven candlesticks in Revelation 1 symbolizes "seven churches", based on what the scripture clearly tells. Yet it symbolizes "the Two Witnesses" in Revelation 11, and again it symbolized the "Menorah" in Zechariah 4.

In Judaism, the menorah symbolizes the divine light that guides and sustains the people of Israel in their relationship with God and their adherence to His commandments.

While the candlestick in Revelation symbolizes the churches and the spiritual light they are called to bear in the world, the Jewish menorah symbolizes God's presence and guidance among the people of Israel. Both depictions carry the themes of light, divine presence, and spiritual illumination, 7 churches, seven branch in grafted within the Menorah. Even though they are applied in different contexts and convey different layers of meaning within their respective religious traditions, the commonality is anointing from God. This is proof that God is for Israel and the Gentiles.

The Two Candlesticks (or Lampstands) that's mentioned in Revelation 11:4 is a part of the apocalyptic vision that conveys that God's "anointed" servants will be empowered by His Spirit to bear witness to His truth. The appearance of the Lampstand and Candlestick in each passage, both for the Jews and Gentiles, each time the Candlesticks or the Lampstand appeared, it denotes "anointed". Or in the case of the seven before the throne, The Anointed One.

This mystery confirms that the Two Witnesses who are already, "standing before the Lord", (the Sun and the Moon), will be the "Two Anointed One" ready for ministry, at that time.

But all things that are reproved are made manifest by the light: for whatsoever doth make manifest is light. Ephesians 5:13

CODED MYSTERIES

John's vision on the Island of Patmos revealed many different coded mysteries that has left many bewildered. Some passages connected to the Old Testament, some in the New Testament, and some would later be revealed, specifically in Revelation. All connecting as parts to the whole truth. While even still, is still left a mystery. For example, the seven stars, seven lampstands, seven church, and the seven spirits.

Different theologians have decoded these mysteries based on what they believe to be factual, and spiritual truths. This writer agrees that interpretation differs, based on many different factors, such as revelation and light.

Revelation 1;4, " John, To the seven churches in the province of Asia: Grace and peace to you from him who is, and who was, and who is to come, and from the seven spirits[a] before his throne, ⁵ and from Jesus Christ, who is the faithful witness, the firstborn from the dead, and the ruler of the kings of the earth. To him who loves us and has freed us from our sins by his blood".

The "seven spirits", is equally interesting and very mysterious. This writer was given partial revelation on this as well, and will discuss more in the future, by God's grace and His mercy, as He directs.

"Turn us again, O LORD God of hosts, cause thy face to shine; and we shall be saved".
Psalm 80:19

✵ CHAPTER 12 SUN-SOAKED AND ANOINTED

"¹¹ For the LORD God is a sun and shield: the LORD will give grace and glory: no good thing will he withhold from them that walk uprightly"
Psalm 84:11

The imagery of the two olive trees is used symbolically to represent God's anointed servants who are empowered by His Spirit to bear witness and accomplish His purposes.

The vision of the two olive trees is described in Revelation 11:4-12, where they are associated with the two witnesses who prophesy and perform miracles during the end times. Olive trees stand tall and soaks up six to 8 hours of sunlight daily in order to produce olives. Without the intense heat and constant direct sunlight, the olive tree cannot be productive, or healthy. This realization further solidifies this writer's theory, that the sun and the moon, are the Two Witnesses that was symbolically mentioned in Revelation as the 2 Olive Trees, and the 2 Lampstand.

Even though they are inanimate, these two luminous witnesses, "stand before the Lord of the earth.", quietly observing, and ready to begin their assignment, as written about in Revelation 11:4.

CHURCH AND MINISTRY

They symbolize divine empowerment, anointing, and spiritual sustenance for those called to be faithful witnesses for God in the midst of adversity. The imagery of the olive trees underscores the themes of divine commission, prophetic ministry, and the endurance of God's servants in the face of opposition.

> "But ye are a chosen generation, a royal priesthood, an holy nation, a peculiar people; that ye should shew forth the praises of him who hath called you out of darkness into his marvellous light"; 1 Peter 2:9

In Revelation, the two olive trees are associated with God's anointed witnesses who testify to His truth and carry out His work during a time of persecution and tribulation. In the context of Revelation, the candlesticks represent the churches or communities of believers, or His ecclesia's who are called to shine the light of God's truth in the world. They symbolize the role of believers as witnesses for Christ and bearers of the gospel message.

The connection between the two olive trees and the two candlesticks suggests a partnership between God's anointed servants (represented by the olive trees) and those called and anointed for service (represented by the candlesticks) in carrying out God's mission on earth. It emphasizes the importance of spiritual empowerment and the proclamation of God's truth by His people.

SYMBOLISM IN JEWISH TRADITION AND CULTURE

The olive tree holds significant symbolism in Jewish tradition, representing themes of peace, prosperity, and divine favor. In the Hebrew Bible (Old Testament), the olive tree is often used metaphorically to depict Israel as God's chosen people or to symbolize spiritual blessings and abundance.

Olive oil, produced from olives, was used for various sacred purposes, such as anointing priests and kings. The menorah, as mentioned in the previous chapter was sacred, and the intent was for the oil to never run out.

Hence the need for a continuous supply of the oil produced by the trees. Zechariahs encounter with the angel, gave clear meaning to validate the need for nonending supply of oil, with the two branches empty the golden oil out of themselves.

"Therefore judge nothing before the time, until the Lord come, who both will bring to light the hidden things of darkness, and will make manifest the counsels of the hearts: and then shall every man have praise of God". 1 Corinthians 4:5

So as the sun produces the heat, the tree produces the olives, and the olive produces the oil, non-ending supply of olive oil. Zechariah 4:12-14

"¹² And I answered again, and said unto him, What be these two olive branches which through the two golden pipes empty the golden oil out of themselves?¹³ And he answered me and said, Knowest thou not what these be? And I said, No, my lord.¹⁴ Then said he, These are the two anointed ones, that stand by the LORD of the whole earth".

Zechariah's encounter with the angel showed one lamp with seven channels, which differed from that in Revelation where John on the aisle of Patmos, witnessed two trees, and two candlesticks in Revelation 11:4 "These are the two olive trees, and the two candlesticks standing before the God of the earth". However, in both cases, both are anointed and brings glory to God.

In the Jewish culture, the olive tree is associated with the land of Israel and its fertility, reflecting God's covenantal relationship with the Jewish people and the promise of His provision and protection. Their enduring nature and ability to produce oil, a symbol of light and purity, are seen as representations of God's faithfulness, nourishment, and favor toward

His chosen people. While the imagery of the olive trees in the Jewish depiction emphasizes themes of blessing, covenant, and divine favor within the context of God's relationship with Israel. It also carries distinct apocalyptic and prophetic significance in Revelation.

"Again, a new commandment I write unto you, which thing is true in him and in you: because the darkness is past, and the true light now shineth". 1 John 2:8

Both depictions highlight the symbolic richness of the olive tree as a powerful symbol of God's anointed vessels ready for ministry, irrespective of whom or what one would believe the Two Witnesses to be.

Both depictions carry spiritual significance in their respective contexts, and in end time prophecy. The 2 Olive trees, and 2 Candlestick or 1 Menorah depicts the universal complete love of God for us all, and shows how much the concepts of engrafting and ingathering of Jews and Gentiles play a significant role in Christian theology and end time prophecy.

"turn night into day; in the face of the darkness light is near". Job 17:12

CHAPTER 13-THE BEAST

Revelation 11:7-13 (NIV):

"**7** Now when they have <u>finished</u> their testimony, the beast that comes up from the Abyss will attack them, and overpower and kill them. **8** Their bodies will lie in the public square of the great city—which is figuratively called Sodom and Egypt—where also their Lord was crucified. **9** For three and a half days some from every people, tribe, language and nation will gaze on their bodies and refuse them burial. **10** The inhabitants of the earth will gloat over them and will celebrate by sending each other gifts, because these two prophets had tormented those who live on the earth.**11** But after the three and a half days the breath[b] of life from God entered them, and they stood on their feet, and terror struck those who saw them. **12** Then they heard a loud voice from heaven saying to them, "Come up here." And they went up to heaven in a cloud, while their enemies looked on **13** At that very hour there was a severe earthquake and a tenth of the city collapsed. Seven thousand people were killed in the earthquake, and the survivors were terrified and gave glory to the God of heaven".

THE BEAST AND THE ABYSS

Throughout the Book of Revelation, the beast symbolizes the forces of evil, persecution, and rebellion that stand in opposition to God and His people.

The beast is bound in religious hatred towards Christ, everyone who accepts Christ, and is accommodating to the systems and practices that hate Christ and His followers, the Anti-Christ system.

"For the commandment is a lamp; and the law is light; and reproofs of instruction are the way of life". Proverbs 6:23

The ascension out of the bottomless pit, as understood by this writer, is that it emerged out of nowhere, or straight out of the crevices of a figurative hell. Since it is not presently active as of today. In fact, it has not emerged yet, because the haters of Christ, are busy fighting amongst themselves. Talk about being blinded.

Interpreting the beast in the Book of Revelation, as well as the mark of the beast, involves understanding the symbolic and apocalyptic nature of the text.

Therefore, you may need to grab your creative, prophetic lens again. Different interpretations exist among theologians and scholars, and views on these symbols can vary based on theological perspectives, historical contexts as with understanding who the Two Witnesses are.

The beast is often interpreted as a physical beast. However, this writer believes the beast to be synonymous to oppressive political systems or rulers that oppose God and persecute believers. It can represent tyrannical governments or empires throughout history that have sought to suppress religious freedom and promote ideologies contrary to the teachings of Christianity. Remember, the beast emerged AFTER the rapture. The mood will be desolate for some, and angry for others who felt tricked in opposing Christ and was left behind.

The powers that be, would have to have some semblance of control, and that could only be maintained through order on a global level. A new world order emerges out of nowhere, out of the "Abyss".

"The people walking in darkness have seen a great light on those living in the land of deep darkness a light has dawned'. Isaiah 9:2

The Word says by the time the Two Witnesses "FINISHED" their testimony, (already after the Rapture), the Christ-haters, or Anti-Christ will begin to come together, and join together to fight one common enemy. As the old saying goes, "An enemy of my enemy, is my friend". So, the haters of Christ, will unite together to fight, what would now be their common and current enemy, at that time. What and Who would be the enemy? That part is not clear if it is a meteorite, the actual physical sun and moon, global warming, global disturbances, or extreme large asteroid. The cosmic disturbances, much like the eclipse, will begin to show the inhabitants of this world, that something has changed, and that God's word is true, and

> most importantly, Christ is real. It's imperative to remember that this phenomenon is taking place AFTER the rapture. So immense fear, uncertainty, grief, and sorrow will be evident across the world. People will know that the Christians were not just being "Bible thumpers", but was teaching truth. Whatever it will be, this will occur only AFTER the sun and the moon has finished their testimony, and thermonuclear weaponry will be used against this perceived and now realized terrorist threat. As stated in Revelation 11 " [7] Now when they have finished their testimony, the beast that comes up from the Abyss will attack them, and overpower and kill them".

. [8] Their bodies will lie in the public square of the great city—which is figuratively called Sodom and Egypt—where also their Lord was crucified. [9] For three and a half days some from every people, tribe, language and nation will gaze on their bodies and refuse them burial. [10] The inhabitants of the earth will gloat over them and will celebrate by sending each other gifts, because these two prophets had tormented those who live on the earth.

[35] Take heed therefore that the light which is in thee be not darkness. Luke 11:35.

This writer believes that it will be at this time, after the shaking of the heavens, that heavenly (celestial) bodies/ objects will be affected and will litter the earth. They cannot be buried. No one will want to touch or move these celestial bodies. They can only "gaze on their bodies", they cannot be touched. People will "refuse" to touch these. The location? The scripture said, where "Christ was crucified", this was in the Middle East.

However, people of all "kindreds, and tongues, and nations" will rejoice and "send each other gifts", They will merry together now after defeating this common threat.

ANTICHRIST

This writer believes the Antichrist is very relevant today, and is not a person but a series of systems, structures, networks, and laws that are formed against Christ. Laws, rules, political organizations, political agendas, and even religion, will be under new scrutiny and new order. Therefore, the Anti-Christ systems and the beast, will work together on a broader scale to create a new world order, that will persecute Christians, oppose God, and seek to undermine His kingdom. It may even be under the guise of doing something beneficial and needed for society on a whole.

People will be forced to publicly acknowledge this new order in order to buy and sell, or live for that matter. Think of individuals that run certain government offices and are corrupt, but this initiative will be on a global scale.

The mark of the beast is public acceptance and allegiance to worldly powers or ideologies that are in opposition to God, by taking the mark.

"And the city had no need of the sun, neither of the moon, to shine in it: for the glory of God did lighten it, and the Lamb is the light thereof". Revelation 21:23

Taking the mark is acceptance and conformity to a godless system and rejection of Christ, for economic gain. Or as some would say for their "survival". This is very telling of the pressure and intense sufferation that will be evident at that time. One would have to take the mark, or choose death.

IF I PERISH, I PERISH

11 And after three days and an half the spirit of life from God entered into them, and they stood upon their feet; and great fear fell upon them which

saw them.[12] And they heard a great voice from heaven saying unto them, Come up hither. And they ascended up to heaven in a cloud; and their enemies beheld them.[13] And the same hour was there a great earthquake, and the tenth part of the city fell, and in the earthquake were slain of men seven thousand: and the remnant were affrighted, and gave glory to the God of heaven.

As to whom, or what the Two Witnesses are, the plan and goal should be to be among those caught up with Jesus when He comes for His church, at the time of Rapture. Not to be here to find out. As we know His coming is very soon, and we out to be ready.

This is in no way to bring gloom and doom. Just to bring awareness, and to be obedient. My prayer is that by releasing what God has shared with me, someone's life will be changed. I thank God for using me, and thank you for your support.

    Shalom

Made in the USA
Columbia, SC
27 August 2024